Re-creations

I·N·S·P·I·R·A·T·I·O·N FROM THE SOURCE

Re-creations

I·N·S·P·I·R·A·T·I·O·N FROM THE SOURCE

Gabriele Lusser Rico

Dedication

For my husband, Richard,
for every teacher who connects,
and
for all my students who blossom into language

> If you search into the question of knowledge, you will find the only things you can be said truly to understand are those you have made yourself..
> —Giambattista Vico

ISBN 1-888842-21-0

Designed by Edward E. Wilson

About the Cover:
The art for the cover is titled *LOVE*. The artist, Costel Iarca, is a native of Romania. Costel Iarca (pronounced *e-arca*) has been painting and sculpting in Chicago for the past five years. His joyful, vibrant work is influenced by moderns such as Picasso, Leger, Matisse, Klee, and Van Gogh (especially his colors). His website is http://home.att.net/~iarca

TABLE OF CONTENTS

Acknowledgments

To neurosurgeon Joseph Bogen, as always.

To my graduate teaching assistants at San Jose State University, who took the ball and ran with Re-creations, especially Kate Evans, Janelle Melvin, Greg Grewell, Andrea Sandke, Cath Hooper, Irina Raicu, Melody Brune, Judy Hobor, Lesley Roberts-Mason, Bobbi Mimmack, Helen Andersson, Francia Stephens, Carol Gerich, Paul Lukes, Thomas Perez-Jewell, Catherine Hooper, Ellen Levy, Shelia Thorne, Catherine Crawford, Jim Micheletti, Cari Johnson, Bret Keeling, Vicky Mendenhall, Emily Wheeler, Stephanie Westphal, Mel Berry, Rebecca Webb, Tiffany Darrough, Dawn Chase, and Mary Bowers.

To students from my Creative Process seminar including Verlene Schermer, Debra Caires, Loretta Naudus, Susanne Tobin, and Robin Nelson.

To the gifted poets in these pages who were the source of our inspiration,

To the members of AEPL, the Assembly on Expanded Perspectives on Learning, for their vision,

To Kate Evans and Janelle Melvin, co-authors with me on Designing Essays

To Roy Anderson of The Demo Shop who helped me shape the voice, the resonance, the sound of the language, so that others can hear it.

And, most especially, to my many students from San Jose State University to my Writing-Intensive participants everywhere (specifically, those at the Omega Institute, Esalen, New York Open Center, and Interface) all of whom experimented, improvised, and played with me and whose wildly divergent Re-creations show how creative human beings can be, given a small creative nudge.

Finally, to Joyce Armstrong Carroll, Edward E. Wilson, and Trey Hall at Absey and Co. who immediately grasped the potential of this book , and who ran with it, and to Andrea Sandke, who commented on the entire manuscript with understanding and empathy and wisdom.

Gabriele Rico
Chicago, IL

FOREWORD

Minds Aquiver

Gabriele Rico has written a compelling book—a gift to teachers and students looking for a way into the imaginal realm where sound and image and mind engender an act of creativity. Her methodology is simple—as in absolute, fundamental.

Those gathered in a classroom or in a workshop begin with a poem, a visual image, or even a snippet of prose. Someone reads a selected text aloud or projects an image on a screen, while others in the room practice the art of listening or seeing. A second reading of the text elicits a *mind map* from each participant—a medley of associations recorded around a blank circle on a sheet of paper. And then, perhaps, a nudge in the direction of meaning—a notion to be jotted in the center of the circle that will account for the recorded associations, something tentative. And finally, a creative task: *In just two and a half minutes re-create what you have just heard or seen, any way you'd like.*

That uncomplicated methodology—derived and tested and expanded by Gabriele for nearly a decade—yields astonishing results, whether used in classroom or workshop. Students, while learning to listen and read, learn also to write. In doing their Re-creations, they go directly to the heart of the creative process. They become agents. Imagining and conceptualizing accompany listening and reading and writing. But students do not have to learn these complex processes one at a time, nor do they have to take them up in a linear sequence. Instead, they experience them simultaneously as they write, under the constricting but liberating impress of time. This process moves the cognitive mind slightly to the side so that uninhibited work can be done with the primary material—the spoken or visual texts.

We find the proof of this methodology in the results—in the work that students have done and in the variations that Gabriele has designed to move students deeper and deeper into cognition and performance. One need only read or view the primary texts (printed throughout the book) and the accompanying student responses to be convinced that this is ground-breaking work, that this is a highly effective and creative way to help students learn to be expressive in writing. To be both expressive and rigorous. To be both personal and academic. To be passionately analytical.

Four years ago in a workshop at the College Conference on Composition and Communication, I experienced the pleasure of such learning as Gabriele read a poem of Sharon Olds about the death of Marilyn Monroe. Those in the workshop enacted the methodology under Gabriele's influence, and, following the two? minutes of writing, there was a spasm of enthusiasm in the room, all of the teachers vying for an opportunity to read what Gabriele and the process had elicited from them. What we read to one another that day left me and others spellbound, eager to get back to our own classrooms.

The first day I tried *Re-creations* in a second-semester writing course, I read only a short passage from a long, complex essay by Clifford Geertz that had been assigned for the day. At the end of two? minutes, I asked for volunteer readers. A young woman's hand shot up, and she gave us a single sentence that captured the essence of Geertz's essay, including subtle details that were enfolded in a sentence worthy of Geertz himself. Others offered their own variations, and by the time the discussion ended, students had a comprehensive understanding of a text that would normally have taken days of discussion to unravel.

On another occasion while working with corporate executives, I read to them Elizabeth Bishop's poem, *Sestina*. My aim was subversive. I asked for a Re-creation, expecting they would stumble over the poem's complexity. They did not. There was more. They gave in return for Bishop poems of their own, drawings, artful sentences, clarity—revealing much of what the poem suggests to us. And yet they missed the intricate, variable form of the sestina. Bishop is so good that the form remains hidden. But as soon as I gave the executives a list of end words from the first two stanzas, they were able to figure out the third and subsequent stanzas. Their creative investment in the Re-creation left them stimulated and eager to continue the workshop in which we were looking into the hidden structures of business organizations. An initial insight led to others—a legacy of images yielding new possibilities.

Gabriele has written a book that will enrich our teaching and our lives. She progresses from her own early experiments to those more complex variations that have continued over the years to yield stunning results for her and others. Along the pathway of that progression, as we follow Gabriele and her students, we sense again and again that the most fundamental exercise can lead to the most astonishing results. We sense as well the vast potential that awaits us in our classrooms, where students come yearning for the lasting satisfaction that accompanies learning. There, in that safe space, students can experience the pleasure of making something of their very own while working under the influence of provocative texts and creative teachers. There, in that space, we can confirm ourselves.

Pat C. Hoy II, Professor of English
Director of Writing Programs
New York University

The Creative Multilogue

As an eleven-year-old immigrant who spoke no English, I recall one thing vividly about the first three months in this strange new country: For some strange reason, I lapsed into virtual silence—I spoke virtually no English and as little German as I could get away with. Looking back, it seems my total mental energy went into listening—really listening—to what is between the lines of language: its tonalities, its emotional spectrum, its rhythms, no matter how little sense its content made to me. I listened to teachers, schoolmates, playmates, neighbors, my own parents trying to speak English when they had to. I recall little pressure on me in those first three months to perform, perhaps because no one much knew what to do with me or knew how to teach me a language that was foreign to my ears. So I spent my time listening, learning gradually to draw some kind of meaning from the welter of sounds assaulting my ear.

> Creativity is like the original flaring forth. It is not judgmental--is not aesthetic--is not critical....Think of creativity as a gift--gift to oneself, gift to others. Not as achievement; not competitive. Like the child who comes running with its latest scribble or mudpie and says SEE WHAT I MADE?
>
> —M. C. Richards

> It is strange to me that we can come to accept the idea that language is primarily learned as speech, is soaked up by osmosis from society by children--but that we then assume the writing down of this flexible language requires a study of linguistics, a systematic checking with lists of standard practices.... My plea is for the value of an unafraid, face-down, flailing, and speedy process in using language
>
> --Wm. Stafford

Why the SOUND of Writing?

When I refer to the sound of writing, people often correct me, you mean *the sound of music.* True, we associate sound with music. True, we associate writing with print. But writing also has to do with the sound and texture and flow of language, articulated by a human voice. Language is also meant to be heard. That's why a CD accompanies this book about writing, improvisation, and creativity. Sound, it turns out, is another way of learning writing. The sound patterns of language which make up a poem, for example, are another way of inviting the would-be writer into surprise, into improvisation, into illumination. Sound—the heard voice, the language voice, the oral tradition, the voiced patterns reconstructed in the listener's ear— is also a way to approach writing. The way a poem sounds influences how the listener understands it, as opposed to reading print on a page.

🔈)) designates that the selection is on the CD.

Even during the first edition of *Writing the Natural Way*, I strongly felt something was missing. It was the element of sound, the heard voice. I have never forgotten a comment made by one of my ESL students at San Jose State University. She said, "When I write my first draft of my essay at home, I remember your voice reading the day' s poem. I hear your voice saying the words I' m writing, and it helps me." Somehow, for her, the unfamiliar language took on resonance, rhythm, and intonation long before the grammar or the words themselves came easily.

The process of Re-creations, the subject of this book, reflects the marriage of the resonant voice and print. We are in the midst of an iconic and aural revolution that began in the nineteenth century with the return of the image. The sound and the images of language— as opposed to the print expressions—are far more democratic, involving more people, enabling more human beings to participate in a multilogue of communication. Even would-be writers who have limited access to language. Even advanced writers who have become mired in its conventions (technical writers, writers of law briefs, of laundry lists), who have forgotten to improvise by playing with language and who want to break free of the blocks into the possibilities of language).

Thus, the primary focus of *Re-creations: Inspiration from the Source* is the diversity of the mind. I want to honor the human mind's multiple abilities to tackle a task. I want to celebrate the human mind's improvisational skills as survival strategies, leading to flexibility and growth of the mind.

This book is a celebration of often untapped creative potential, of the power of improvisation, and what I am after in the listener is that the *spectator* become more than a just a spectator, more than just a reader, more than just a listener but a participant in the creative act. I am after shifts, departures from the original, veering into one's own mental territory emotional territory, linguistic territory. I am after tapping into the instability that characterizes the creative human mind, leading to fluctuation, variation, after the hunches, guesses, configurations of the purely *schooled* mind. I am after connecting the created artifact with the personal.

I want the created artifact , something already made by another human being, to hover and hang fire in the listening mind, tapping into global feelings, into the human need to create patterns of meaning, into understanding at the deepest level. Meaning-making is ultimately an indeterminate process with random variables which cannot be eradicated. Let us make use of that uncertainty.

> My aim is to show that the writing is simple, if it is done by the swimming-in-itself technique; but that in analyzing the writing we can make it appear almost impossibly difficult.
>
> —William Stafford

Entering into a Re-creation is a way of paying attention to language in a different way because the listener is not only listening, she will DO something with what she has just heard—in this moment. Re-creation is about listening not just to any language, but language at its most powerful, most compressed, most evocative, in short, poetry. It is improvising— on the spot—to make a personal pattern of meaning of it—all in a very brief time span. This re-creative act both activates and marries aural and visual pathways in the brain as they tackle the improvisational task together, leading to an exponential leap toward meaning. And to surprise. And to immense pleasure. And to a product. And to a sense of accomplishment.

Since I began experimenting with Re-creations eight years ago, I noticed that the act of listening to something read aloud and then re-creating it in one's own way in minutes, consistently produced amazing results at all ages, reminding me of Paul Klee's statement that "experiencing the works of others is like experiencing nature."

Key Characteristics of Re-creations:

· The heard poem seems to trigger a scanning for relevant elements rather than a sequence.

· Context is king: poem and the listener' s images are relational.

· Re-creation forges an immediate, personal connection to the created poem.

· The rhythms of sound and voice and words influence attention to nuance.

· A unique and unpremeditated form evolves.

· Resonance of voices—yours and the poet's together—produce something different from the original, bringing into question the old issue of plagiarism versus borrowing and synthesis.

· Active quiescence in listening is transformed into a dynamic creative act of writing.

· Empowerment—language becomes a pool of all the voices which we hear, have heard, will hear, and can tap into—a multilogue.

Poet Heather McHugh , in her book, *Broken English*, argues that poetry often begins with—and is characterized by—fragments: " All poetry is fragment. It is shaped by its breakages at every turn, " the advertent and the inadvertent. We begin with a phrase, Begin not with idea or intention but rather with phrase, sentence, sound. "

The recent signals from the teaching Academy—that we need to look at different, more creative ways of teaching writing—are multiple: Wendy Bishop , in *Crossing the Lines; On Creative Composition and Composing Creative Writing* argues for synthesis. Santos Sherod, in his *American Poetry Review* essay , argues that "poetic thought is to think away from what the poet knows best, and toward that which is unthinkable" and insists that "the poem revises the poet, not the other way around!" He urges writers to write about "what you know the least, about that which you find the most unthinkable." The AEPL—Assembly on Expanded Perspectives on Learning—a recognized sub-group of the NCTE and CCCC, has been most active and has a journal, the JAEPL, which addresses issues of going beyond our present ideas, practices, and beliefs about how to teach writing to learners who desperately need to feel at home with language. This book strives to substantiate their insights, strives to enfold more learners in the excitement of writing—and strives to help would-be writers to write successfully.

The FORMAT of the Book

· **The Emerging Theory** of creativity here is substantiated by the writings of many who have gone before me, by the many examples, by the description of the process of Re-creations, and by the conclusions drawn about the differences between borrowing and synthesis.

· **The student examples** of Re-creations form the heart of each chapter, preceded and followed by what I have come to understand about this amazing process.

· **The quotations** illuminate, reflect, and intensify the often not easily identifiable or verbalizable aspects of the process of Re-creations. Sprinkled throughout , they underscore he tacit understanding of many that much learning is implicit instead of explicit

· **The student comments** came from three written questions asked at the end of a Re-creation: " I was surprised…I discovered…I wonder…." These questions help learners to become aware of their own processes.

· **The layout** of the original poems and the Re-creations the poems spawned is more like a cluster than a sequence, with the original poem in the center and the Re-creations arranged around it with arrows. This layout honors the original for its power to motivate and it honors the diverse responses which become their own expression of the original.

> People are always talking about originality; but what do they mean? As soon as we are born, the world begins to work upon us, and this goes on to the end. What can we call our own except energy, strength, and will? If I could give an account of all that I owe to great predecessors and contemporaries, there would be a small balance in my favor.
>
> —Johann Wolfgang von Goethe, 1 825

The CENTRAL ISSUES of the Book

· **The Issue of Creativity:** Creative acts do not belong only to the very few. It is a hallmark of the human mind, a way of moving beyond where we are at the present moment. It needs to be tapped, and it needs to be illuminated.

· **The Issue of Borrowing vs. Synthesis:** Often, what teachers have called plagiarism is just that— words, sentences, paragraphs, essays copied word for word and passed off as one' s own. In Re-creation something different happens: First, it is heard as the created artifact is filtered through ear, then through the experiential sieve of each mind. Second, it is transformed into something new and unique as the hearer DOES something with the listening. A Re-creation is not a paraphrase; it is not a copy; it is not plagiarized, nor is it mere imitation. Because it is its own configuration, we must look at the central role of a learner's being able to *stand on the shoulders of giants* in order to discover his/her own voice and thereby, to learn and grow.

> Everything has been thought of before, but the problem is to think of it again.
>
> —Johann Wolfgang von Goethe

> I believe that our aesthetic sense, whether in works of art or in lives, has overfocused on the stubborn struggle toward a single goal rather than on the fluid, the protean, the improvisatory. The landscape through which we move is in constant flux. Children cannot even know the names of the jobs and careers that will be open to them; they must build their fantasies around temporary surrogates. Goals too clearly defined can become blinkers.
> —M.. C. Bateson

• The Issue of Technology and the Iconic Revolution, given its Impact on Reading, Writing, and Thought: Leonard Shlain notes that the amount of time people spend watching images flit on a screen have surpassed the amount of time people spend reading linear rows of black letters. Comprehending images requires different strategies from those used in reading.

The iconic revolution means that we honor and reward not only the print equivalents of knowledge, such as IQ tests, SAT scores, essay exams, demonstrations of thesis, topic sentence, power statements, definitive conclusions, but the moving image and the resonant voice as vehicles of extending the boundaries of one's knowings. It means that we honor not only the analytic, the alphabetic, the sequential, the print, but that we honor other ways of making sense of the world—the sounds, movements, and images reflective of language which have taken a back seat to the print medium for 250 years in formal learning. Voice and image are ambiguous, ambivalent resonant, recapitualitive, re-creative. Since we do not yet know how to test for this aspect of language, we cannot honor it.

A heart-felt thanks goes to the many, many students who played and experimented and risked each time we re-created. If their voices are anonymous, it is only because there was no intention to write a book about Re-creations and, over the years, their names were not printed on the daily handouts I created of their two and a half-minute improvisations, the results of each Re-creational activity. Students knew they would be represented on one handout or another in the course of the semester, and they could announce themselves if they so chose as we read them aloud and discussed them. Most students were simply—and quietly—proud. All knew they had a voice. All knew their voice mattered and that each voice was a part of the multilogue that made them genuine participants in learning, in writing improvisationally, and in creative acts, Their voices resonate on these pages as testimony to the creative human spirit.

> Jazz exemplifies artistic activity that is at once individual and communal, performance that is both repetitive and innovative, each participant sometimes providing background support and sometimes flying free.
> —M.C. Bateson

> Science, like art, is not a copy of nature but a recreation of her. We remake nature by the act of discovery, in the poem or in the theorem.
> —J. Bronowski

Andrea Sandke, one of my former students, muses: "When we're given poems to re-create, it's almost as if we're given something as powerful as a mathematical theorem—only, instead of being told there is *one* correct answer, we get to explore the theorem, plant it in the ground, as it were, to let it grow into something other—and potentially alive."

All of us, in some way or another, have to learn over and over how to communicate in language, and although it is more comfortable when we imagine that there are right answers—it is a more powerful thing to learn how to work with the unknown. And listening, and trusting one's instincts—these are perhaps the best tools to deal with that unknown.

In the course of writing this book, having thought much about Re-creations and the power of listening, I suddenly realize that my inexplicable silence during those first months in a strange country with strange language sounds was eminently constructive: I learned to listen—really listen—to sounds and pauses and tonality, to image, idea, and idiom, and most of all, to the emotional timbre of the new language I was suddenly immersed in. Not only did I learn to find my voice again, but this experience has helped me understand the frequent muteness of students, and would-be-writers, actual writers, and just plain people who are afraid to fail. I want to give each of them the knowledge that they can write in living, breathing, meaningful language—in language meaningful to them. I also want them to remember to listen—not for the *right* response, but for whatever a piece might have to offer—and then to share, to be included and not be ashamed for having spoken truthfully. For myself, in learning to listen, I learned to say what I need to say—again and again. In learning to speak this language in those silences, I also learned to love it passionately enough to want others to love it, too.

CHAPTER ONE

The Resonant Voice

CREATION AND RE-CREATION

> Creativity has not only made the human race unique in Nature; what is more important, it gives value and purpose to human existence.
>
> —J.E. and Glenda Bogen

Who is Creative?

> Combinatory play seems to be the essential feature in productive thought.
>
> —Einstein

Many of us wonder at one time or another why other people are creative while we are not, why other people have ideas and we do not, why some can write and we do not. I know I have. What I didn't know for the longest time, perhaps didn't understand or or trust—is that—all human beings have an built-in potential for creative acts. As small children we play, analogize, listen, guess, imitate, borrow, are surprised, ask, pretend, generalize, imagine, try, fail, try again, try on, are curious, delight in, and, above all, are not yet interested in the *correct* answer—we do not as yet know it exists.

Learners as Observers, as Participants, as Creators:

Throughout our lives, as learners, we shift among three fundamental roles: as observers, as participants, and as creators. As observers, we are like an audience at a concert, primarily taking in the given performance of others. As participants, we are like the members of the orchestra, performing as one of a group to bring the music to life. As creators, we are like the composer of the piece performed by the orchestra and watched by the audience.

As we grow and learn, we are sometimes observers, sometimes participants, and sometimes creators. We can learn from all three roles, although in formal schooling learners are more often passive than active. I found that the more often learners can be active *participants* and *creators* in addition to being observers, the more intense a learning experience becomes.

One of the impediments to the learner's role as participant or creator has been the romantic ideal of the artist as the lone genius and the rest of humanity as incapable of such creative acts. In his extensive essay, *The Translated Image*, British artist Michael Ayrton noted that "the creation of any work of art, however great and however original, is dependent [on] precedents in the memory." Pointing out that all great artists, from Michelangelo, Titian, Leonardo, Raphael, and the Impressionists, to the giants of modernism, like Cezanne and Picasso, borrowed incessantly, he also insists that such borrowings were also part of their vitality. "The act of power," he wrote, "lies in the attempt to do again, to recreate, an image ..." Analyzing such *copying*, he draws the conclusion that "the copyist is in the act of questioning, examining, accepting, and discovering the thought of his predecessor" and that "the most natural thing to do [is] to go to the sources, to the already established images." In responding to predecessors in this way, he notes, "a vital cross fertilization took place...the adaptation of individual parts of one artist's picture to another artist's purposes."

> To compare a great copy with a great original is to attend a conversation between great artists.
> —Michael Ayrton

I wanted to find ways to enable students to play more than their often passive roles. I wanted to see learners as participants—even better—as creators, of their own learning. To become participants, they had to DO things with their learning beyond taking tests. To become creators, they had to be given the opportunity to move into uncharted territory in DO-ing something with the learning to generate their own unique emerging patterns of meaning. So I began to experiment, and this book shows what happens when learners become creators, when learning becomes a creative act. This book explores, with first-hand examples, how the creative acts are sparked. It reminds us all that we are not *tabula rasas* but that we relearn the most important things in life over and over, yet each time in new ways, from new angles, in new contexts.

Combinatory Play

> If you search into the question of knowledge, you will find the only things you can be said truly to understand are those you have made yourself.
> —Giambattista Vico

The creative process relies on combinatory meaning-seeking. We build on—and we alter—what we encounter in our built-in search for meaning. We want to move beyond where we are now to reach for something more, something that satisfies our mind's need for meaningful patterns. The creative process is nothing more than a previously unrecognized opportunity. It relies on the flexibility to connect new experience and prior knowledge. And it relies on surprise: the ability to be startled into an emotional connection between what is now and what was. Finally, it relies on that emotional *impetus* (L. *motus* to move), to make this involvement palpable in some form—to *real-eyes* it in some medium. Therefore, one way to activate creative moments is to surprise or startle the mind into it. Creative acts cannot be imposed, only invited.

Improvisation is a discovery process, yet not one of us creates in a vacuum; we are affected by the creations of others, not to mention our own past knowledge, skill, experience, emotions. Because meaning-seeking is fueled by affect, we take in only those patterns outside of us which are meaningful to our unique expanding inner world-map, and eliminate those that are not. Creative leaps occur in us when we suddenly contextualize incoming information in new and surprising ways. In my experience, I have seen that the surprise into feelings contextualizes thought, ideas, images. When we are startled into surprise, we are emotionally moved to pull internal experience to the surface and to connect it to something external, something new to be learned. This emotional hook reorganizes the new input with the experiences we've already integrated, giving shape to the multiplicity of experience. Shaping helps us to become clear about our inner needs. The emerging pattern stands for who and what

> Few great inventions or observations of experience have long gone unimitated and few therefore have long gone undeveloped.
> —Michael Ayrton

we are in the moment, for how and why we feel in the present. Because we are essentially creative and because we need to define ourselves by our own creative leaps, we seek meaning by constant reorganization. And so improvisation makes of us bricoleurs who preempt all which will help us make meaning for ourselves.

The Making of Meaning

Each time we recombine, we expand on who we are, what we desire, how we see things. Psychiatrist and futurist Charles Johnston says that the palpable expression of our learning is not an appendix to knowing but the way by which something becomes knowing. The dynamic human brain delights in its leaps to connect with the thoughts of others. As creators we simultaneously spiral both inward and outward, inward to discover our own identity, outward by transcending ourselves to discover meaning, choosing seemingly discontinuous aspects of the world that cohere because of our primal impulse to make that world meaningful to ourselves.

Listening

When we are asked to express, in our own way, something we have heard we begin to listen differently, with a different kind of attention that enables us to connect our internal and external world maps. Listening and actually *doing* something with what we have heard, activates combinatory play. So, being creative is coming out to dance on a slippery floor. Unfortunately, as adults, many of us think we must wait for the accidental creative spark just as our ancestors had to wait for lightning to strike in order get fire. We cannot command the creative. One way to invite it is to use others' creative artifacts to spark the creative within us.

Let's take a poem read aloud. We can hear it, listen sporadically, be bored, think of something else, be confused, think that we don't like poetry, or any combinations thereof. However, listening to something read because we know we will DO something with the created pattern of someone else's mind—changes the quality of our listening. Our minds, because it can't grasp all the details, shifts into almost a sideways attention, not trying too hard, but just being receptive begins to engage in mental combinatory play. When this combinatory play is caught in words on a page, making this mental play visible, something clicks in us. That click opens the door to improvisation.

> Set free, the mind discovers shortcuts and arabesques through and over and around all purposes. . . Would a pattern emerge? Yes, it would. Do you have to be careful to make a meaningful pattern emerge? No.
>
> —Wm. Stafford

My husband, an orthopedic surgeon who often jokes that he "took humanities once," was certain he would not—could not—produce anything creative, no matter what. In a workshop setting, he listened to the following poem by Adrienne Rich read aloud, knowing the rest of the group would be writing something, not intending to write himself. To his great surprise, he found himself writing a Re-creation. To his great delight, his mind began to make leaps of association to his great passion, photography. He was not only sparked into a creative act but elated by the uniqueness of the piece he had generated in a short time. Here is the original poem he heard:

Dissolve in Slow Motion

Alicia Suskin Ostriker

When you watch a marriage
Dissolve, in slow motion,
like a film, there is a point
Early on when the astute
Observer understands nothing
Can prevent the undesired
End, not shrinks, or friends,
Or how-to-love books,
Or the decency or the will
Of the two protagonists
Who struggle gamely like lab
Mice dropped in a jar
Of something viscous: the
Observer would rather snap
The marriage like a twig,
Speed the suffering up, but
The rules of the lab forbid.

Other rules govern decay
From within; so she just watches:
The little paws claw
Then cease, the furred
Bubbles of lungs stop.
The creatures get rigid.
Has something been measured?
It all gets thrown away!

And here, in a short amount of time, his combinatory mind led him to *hold* what struck him in the moment by simply clustering words and phrases around a circle left blank, then naming the center, which was *photography*, then quickly writing the following vignette:

Photography
Another day in the darkroom lab—
A marriage of black and white.
Viscous fluids,
        measured chemicals,
                dissolving bubbles.

In the end,
another perfect
photographic
                print.

—Richard Ressman

This is a perfect example of one mind's potential to express its own unique pattern, reflecting its interests in this moment of listening, yet influenced by someone else's piece just heard.

Listening to someone else's pattern of meaning evokes images which expand our own ever-shifting, ever-growing minds. When we tap these images in improvisational ways, we are surprised into expressiveness.

Art as a Meetingplace:

Any work of art is brought to completion only when it becomes a meeting-place of two or more minds, when a connection is made between minds. The connecting process has to do less with logical grasp than with what we understand AT THE MOMENT it is experienced, and only when it is experienced.

Most of us, though we are in awe of the creative, suffer from a set of ingrained beliefs which prevent us from even trying to—let alone thinking that we could—be creative. One of these beliefs is that we cannot borrow from, or build on, the creative products of others. Many great artists, for example, Michelangelo and Picasso, did not suffer from such beliefs. As a young man, Picasso haunted museums. He pored over the images and creative ideas of others and took inspiration from the source, that is from the creative expressions of others. In so doing, he reinterpreted (reinvented, recreated, reorganized reassembled) what he found there, in the process developing his own expressive powers. Still he haunted museums. By the time he was fifteen, he could paint like Velasquez or Delacroix. Even then he haunted museums. Gradually, he began to transcend the great painters that had gone before him, but he incorporated many of their images and ideas in an on-going search for his own. Even as a mature painter he continued to haunt museums to keep learning, exploring, and transcending what he saw. In fact, any highly creative people readily admit they stood on the shoulders of the giants who had gone before. This inspiration from the source becomes a feedback loop between what has gone before and what is emergent in an individual. The result is what Albert Einstein called *combinatory play*, moving from the known into the unknown. Such combinatory looping leads to creative acts.

The Two Sides of the Brain: The Role of the Corpus Callosum in Creative Acts

For thirty-five years now we have read and heard about the two sides of the brain. Creativity, according to pioneer split-brain surgeon, Joseph Bogen, demands the highest and most elaborate activities of the brain, requiring the cooperation of the talents of both hemispheres. The "specialization of the hemispheres for different trains of thought greatly increases the flexibility of the ensemble," writes Bogen. Having two modes of thought segregated is advantageous since it will increase the prospects to find solutions to novel situations.

The right hemisphere focuses on the melody, the big picture, while the left hemisphere focuses on the notes, or the sequences, the particulars. Any creative act involves intense activity of both sides of the brain, specifically hemispheric cooperation. This fact has pushed researchers like Bogen to look more closely at the role of the corpus callosum in creative acts.

Bogen argues that the creative moment does not depend on one hemisphere or the other (the right side is often erroneously labeled as the *creative* side of the brain), but on heightened communication between the two hemispheres. This is where the corpus callosum, that connective band of 200 million nerve fibers serving as the bridge between the two hemispheres, comes in. The corpus callosum's central location and its large size has been puzzling students of the brain for centuries. A quick summary of two key points:

- the corpus callosum acts as both gateway and gatekeeper in deciding what is to go through.;
- the corpus callosum is the structure by which the two hemispheres not only shar, but profit by each others' unique way of processing input.

> When we mistrust [intuition] or let it atrophy. . . we end up tuning in with mono to a stereo world.
> —Philip Goldberg

The greater the flexibility of the brain and the greater the quality of interhemispheric transfer, the greater the potential of an individual to be surprised into a creative act. Although flexibility also presupposes greater instability, Bogen speculates that, "the successful expansion of the human species (so far) suggests that the loss of stability is less important than the gain in flexibility."

> Irregularity, chaos lead to complex systems. It's not at all disorder. I would say that chaos is what makes life possible. The brain has been selected to become so unstable that the smallest effect can lead to the formation of order.
>
> —Ilya Prigogine, physicist

Inspiration and Emotion

A moment of inspiration or surprise is dependent on destabilization and the feeling that accompanies it. Mathematician Henri Poincaré, in trying to puzzle out his own creative process, said that inspiration—sudden awareness of the big picture—were important points of departure for expression. Since inspiration is linked to a heightening of affect, the brain is momentarily thrown into turbulence, which may result in a flash of combinatory play which would not otherwise have happened. Surprise is central to learning leaps. This sense of flash of surprise usually triggers a desire to express or examine something in greater detail. Composer Paul Hindemith describes the phenomenon as follows:

> We all know the impression of a heavy flash of lightning in the night. Within a second's time we see a broad landscape. . . . We experience a view, immensely comprehensive and at the same time immensely detailed, that we could never have under normal daylight conditions, if our senses and nerves were not strained by the extraordinary suddenness of the event.

Creative Process as Multilogue:

Creativity not only depends on how the two sides of our brains dialogue with each other, it equally depends on how we communicate with the ideas of others. As a teacher, I wondered: "How can I show learners that they shape their world as much as they are shaped by it? How can I startle them into improvisation so that their own creative leaps become palpable and visible on a page? How can I help learners see that, their approach to the acts, facts, and artifacts of the world makes them creators of their own learning? How can I teach learners to transcend their present learning to incorporate the new in unconventional ways?"

> What does it mean to be released into language? Not simply learning the jargon of the expected but learning that language can be used as a means of changing reality. What interests me in teaching is less the emergence of the occasional genius than the discovery of language by those who did not have it.
>
> —A. Rich

What emerged was a truly stunning evocative

process I now call *Re-creations*. I knew I was after something of potential revolution when I came across a German experiment with visual art which was analogous to what I was imagining with words. This German museum's experiment involved children in active seeing —that is, they were asked to DO something with what they had viewed instead of passively looking and going on to something else.

Visual Re-creations: The German Experiment

> Expression is not an appendix to knowing but an integral part of the process by which something becomes knowing.
>
> —Charles M. Johnston, M.D.

The docents of the Kunstinstitut in Frankfurt, Germany, unhappy with inattentive children, gave a group of children from four to fourteen two specific tasks: 1) To be selective: to choose their favorite painting from many as they walked through a collection; 2) To paint —*from memory*—that work in any way they wished or were able.

After children chose their favorite painting, they were led into a basement with supplies and were asked to paint or draw the painting they had chosen—*from memory*. The museum was experimenting to see whether there would be a shift in the quality of children's attention from passive to active and whether children could follow through with their own rendering of what they had seen.

They didn't have to be asked twice. Once before an easel in the basement of the museum, the students painted with abandon. They were allowed to bring with them only what they remembered. This memory seemed affect-linked, as though they had a stake in it. They painted with fervor—often honing in on a feeling, a special angle, or some ineffable quality on which they focused with intuitive certainty.

> The act of creation engages us all—the composition of our lives. Each of us has worked by improvisation, discovering the shape of our creation along the way, rather than pursuing a vision already defined.
>
> —Mary Catherine Bateson

Figure 1.2

Figure 1.1

For example, five year-old Sara re-creates Lovis Corinth's *Carmencita* (Figs. 1.1 & 1.2), expressing the qualities of redness/blackness, whiteness in a lushly red-lipped snowman. Ice was the dominant impression Sara had in the prominent white chest and the haughtly stare of Carmencita. Children paint what they understand in some way—painting it reflects HOW they understand it.

Five-year-olds Simon Pak and Ariadne Cheropoulou (Fig. 1.3) are captivated by Roelant Savery's *Orpheus unter den Tieren* (Fig. 1.4); what they recall together is the powerful elephant that is actually in the far background of the original and almost undetectable. The lion moves position and direction, and the Orpheus figure disappears altogether. Simon and Ariadne focus on the familiar animals.

Figure 1.4

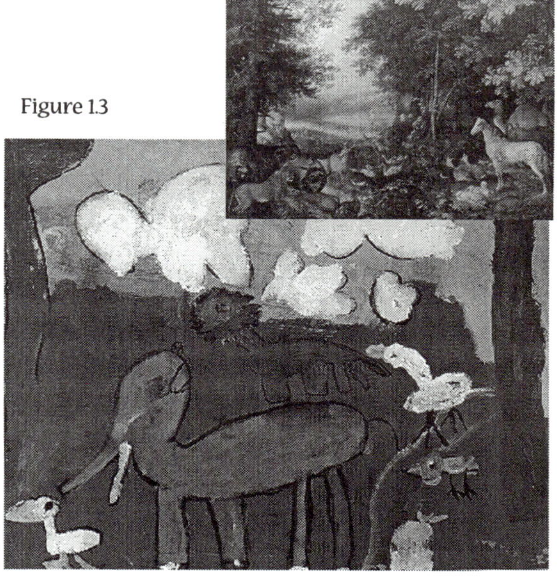

Figure 1.3

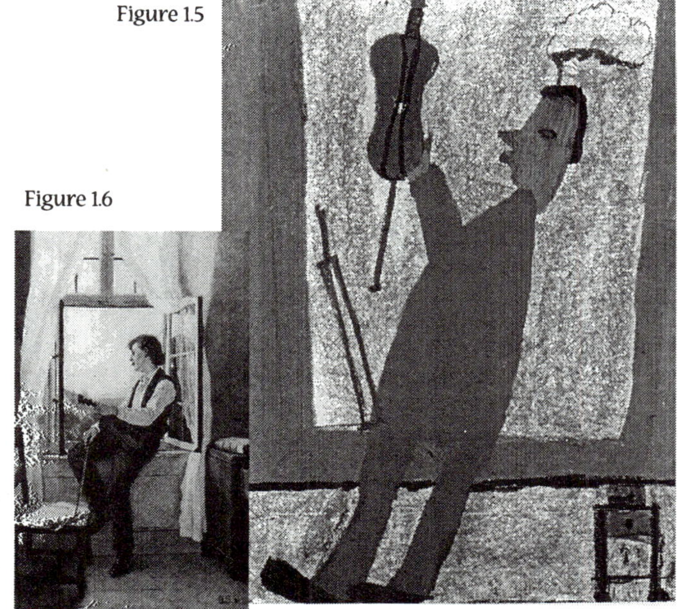

Figure 1.5

Figure 1.6

Five-year-old Johannes Seifert (Fig. 1.5) re-created Otto Franz Scholderer's *Der Geiger am Fenster* (Fig. 1.6) expressing the qualities of intense blues not found in the originial. Probably the most striking element of Johannes' re-creation is he shows a thought bubble of what the musician is thinking about (rolling green hills) while playing the violin. His rendering becomes his own unique creation!

What I saw in this German experiment at the time was three-fold:

- We bring the design mind's natural patterning propensity to a created artifact. The re-creators filter the image through their own experiential sieve and generate what is meaningful and do-able in the present.
- The children do not copy; they do not imitate but re-create—in the absence of the model— the original.
- Thus, Re-creation means just that: to make again in new combination. There is no such thing as a *correct* way to do it; there is no judgment of *better* or *worse*; there are no rules about how much to repeat or not repeat. Thus, re-creating becomes a qualitative effort, not a duplicating effort.

Verbal Re-creations:

I thought, "how can I bring the immediacy of this process to language? The next day in my university class, I said to my students, "Today, we're going to improvise. I'll read a poem aloud. Listen to it. Simply listen, be receptive, enjoy the melody of it. When I read the same piece a second time, pull any words or phrases without plan or effort by jotting them down *around* a blank circle (Inverse Clustering). When I finish the second reading, ask yourself, "What does my center want to be called (a dominant impression, a feeling, your own title, the actual title)" ? Write this in the center of the circle, then re-create whatever wants to come. If you are at a loss for words, glance at your cluster. There is no *right* or *wrong* way to re-create, so just be open to mind-play, be curious about what turns up." Somewhat hesitantly I told them they would have three minutes to improvise,.

They listened, heard, processed, listened a second time, heard, clustered around a blank circle on their page, wrote for three minutes, and named their Re-creation. I collected their papers and took them home to read. I was stunned at their improvisations. Let me share one of the first poems I read, accompanied by several randomly chosen Re-creations by eighteen year-olds:

The original:

Hood

C. K Williams

Remember me? I was the one
In high school you were always afraid of.
I kept cigarettes in my sleeve, wore
engineer's boots, long hair, my collar
up in back and there were always
girls with me in the hallways.
You were nothing. I had it in for you—
when I peeled rubber at the lights
you cringed like a teacher.
And when I crashed and broke both lungs
on the wheel, you were so relieved
that you stroked the hard Ford paint
and your hands shook.

The Re-creations:

He Was Cool

He was cool, he
always picking on me. Thought he
had me scared. I wasn't scared.
I just didn't like him.
Well, he could have the sleazy girls
and the lung cancer
and all the shallow glory from their
stupidity.
Yeah—I might have been square,
doing what was so-called right.
But my mother was proud of me
and me of myself
I was still the one in the race.
And I won:
I'm still alive.

Misfits

They didn't fit,
got into trouble, asked questions.
I wished I'd been that brave, that knowing.
Later I learned to cuss,
to trespass a
& find the swimming hole—
and what it felt like to
batter my fragile wings against
the bars.

Who's Afraid?

You think you're so cool with your
long hair and cigarettes.
You hide behind your engineer's boots,
and those girls in the hall, they mean nothing.
You are the one afraid,
afraid of high school
afraid of hallways
afraid of being you.
Oh, you make me cringe, and I feel relief
because I am not you.

The Girl Who Wanted Out

The freaks and the jocks
had it in for each other.
I was neither,
just a plain girl who wanted out,
way out.
I had nothing to offer anyone then.
I was a mere child forced into a mold
I was not capable of conforming to.
I was not pretty, or thin, or rich.
But I was there, freaks & jocks,
you just don't remember.

Exploring the Process:

Amazingly, all students had been startled into writing. All had re-created a pattern of meaning; all had shown an astounding grasp of some essence of the heard piece, a poem they had only heard twice and had never seen in print. Yet each Re-creation took its own idiosyncratic shape each retained some connection to the original. I typed several Re-creations onto a single page—whatever would fit on a single page along with the original. At the next class meeting we read these aloud. Students were as astonished—and delighted—as I was with their creative expressions. Our discussion of the process yielded the following:

- that each voice in these Re-creations was unique and had personalized the original in one way or another.
- that the voices in the Re-creation usually spoke in the first person, as though they were responding to the *Hood.*
- that some voices brought another angle of vision, such as the girl's voice who sees herself caught between the two worlds of *freaks* and *jocks,* unnoticed.

Over the course of a number of experiments, I saw that 1) a Re-creation rarely required more than three minutes. 2) it built improvisationally on a text read aloud, the inspiration from a source of the title of this book. 3) this process seemed to activate the mind's pattern-seeking predilection, generating loose linkages of words and ideas. 4) Re-creations are expressed in an absurdly brief time span, leading me to the conclusion that, the longer we have to worry about what we should write, might write, could write, if only…, the more chance we have of doubting our melody-recognition, the greater the likelihood of contracting into the *I can't* syndrome, and the more we shut ourselves off from our creative potential.

Let's look at a second set of Re-creations inspired by David Wagoner's *The Old Words.*

The Old Words
David Wagoner

This is hard to say
Simply, because the words
Have grown so old together:
Lips and eyes and tears,
Touch and fingers
And love, out of love's language,
Are hard and smooth as stones
Laid bare in a streambed,
Not failing or fading
Like the halting speech of the body
Which will turn too suddenly
To ominous silence,
But like your lips and mine
Slow to separate, our fingers
Reluctant to come apart,
Our eyes and their slow tears
Reviving like these words
Springing to life again
And again, taken to heart,
To touch, love, to begin.

New Vision
Why did I get caught up in those familiar things,
mundane things that have lost all novelty.
There is nothing new. Why?
Why not let my imagination soar
or listen to the nightingale's song
and wander off with him,
like others do, into the dark?
—Not into the breath-constricting darkness
but one offering a new vision,
no stagnant air
no dark shadows.
Only a welcoming night
which lets me become one with it
and sense things differently.
A new vision. Yes,
that's it,
a new vision.

Words, Words, and Words

How many times can you rearrange the same words over and over in endless combination? How many times will these same words evoke the desired emotions, wring yet more blood from the stone? If words have power, do the same words have the same power again and again in someone else's mouth? How many ways is it possible to say the birds glide over windswept cliffs? I'm going WORD-CRAZY FROM ENDLESS ROUNDS OF WRITING, ALWAYS HAVING TO MAKE IT COME OUT NEW! HELP ME! I'M FALLING

INTO
THIS
GREAT
WORD
VORTEX
AS I
WRITE
MY WAY
UP
INTO
MY OWN
MIND

A Memory

Snow on the ground, the girls wearing
cold stiff levis under their short dresses,
we made our way into the country school house.

Outside a thin wind creaked the windmill,
a black crow settled in the merry-go-round,
and the door was shut firmly on the world outside.

Inside we opened our books. A second-grade reader.
And from it poured forth stories of wonder:
The two Chinese brothers with blousy red trousers &
golden sandals. How enthralled we sat, our minds
soaking up the miracle of one brother swallowing up
a foreign sea for the other to fish.
How we gripped the hard back cover,
waiting as the brother's face grew red,
waiting while the other brother picked up the fish from
the dry lake.
And then,
too late.
The lake filled up
with water. And our hearts stopped.
Too terrible. Too exciting. How could we
ever pass the crow again without feeling loss?

Wind over Water

Wind over water shines
as I count the days.
Life continues around me,
while I, in my misery,
wait, though I don't know
for what.

Wind over water shines,
blurring the water into soothing
motion
while I stare
and find all around me
motionless and still.
Still, all life continues around me.

Struggling with Words

Word by word I strain and struggle
to release them
to get them out of me,
to free my mind like
a bowel movement frees a body,
almost there, a little more:
PUSH
Ahh! Finally
the words drop out
relieving
built-up pressure.
I begin to write.

Words Everywhere

The air is full of words,
the wind rushing roughly over stones
and through meadows
the birds in their nests
singing the old songs
year
after
year
the light beating smoothly
on earth and stones
has its words
year after year.
We hear the words
until we grow old
and die.
The air will still be full
of words
after we are gone.

Words in Time

The more I read
the more thoughts, pictures
melt into each other.
I am not sovereign, just
created by
the grasses, the mountains,
the winds, the same sun
known by others
before me.
These words tie time together
and I
continue to tie the knots,
one by one,
in repetition,
now and then inventing a new knot,
saying the same things
until I pass the job
to someone else.

The Unbearable Lightness of Words

The old words
are like old thoughts,
past moments whispering from trees;
they never quite disappear
just repeat themselves,
different voices
the same notes
whirling, chasing the wind's song.

Comment: Wagoner's poem is an amazing artifact—because of the words, words, words—to observe the impact of Re-creations. Not only does each individual consciousness do its own thing— each generation of readers does its own thing. I read this poem a number of years ago, and the emotional impact of the poem was radically different from the emotional impact I experience today, here, now. The *old words* of David Wagoner, for each Re-creator, circling and cycling in each consciousness, become contextualized and therefore cannot help but be different for each individual. Each sees only the feedback loop compatible with his/her experience. At the same time, each re-creator generates a new context for those words, for the ideas embedded in those words, for the emotional link of those words, for the evolving story-pattern of those words. Thus, the creative act, inspired by a source, becomes totally its own.

Let's look at a longer original and the Re-creations inspired by it

Writing in the Dark

Denise Levertov

It's not difficult.
Anyway, it's necessary.

Wait till morning, and you'll forget.
And who knows if morning will come.

Fumble for the light, and you'll be
stark awake, but the vision
will be fading, slipping
out of reach.

You must have paper at hand,
a felt-tip pen, ballpoints don't always flow,
pencil points tend to break. There's nothing
shameful in that much prudence: those are our tools.

Never mind about crossing your t's, dotting your i's—
but take care not to cover
one word with the next. Practice will reveal
how one hand instinctively comes to the aid of the other
to keep each line
clear of the next.

Keep writing in the dark;
a record of the night, or
words that pulled you from depths of unknowing,
words that flew through your mind, strange birds
crying their urgency with human voices,

or opened
as flowers of a tree that blooms
only once in a lifetime:

words that may have the power
to make the sun rise again

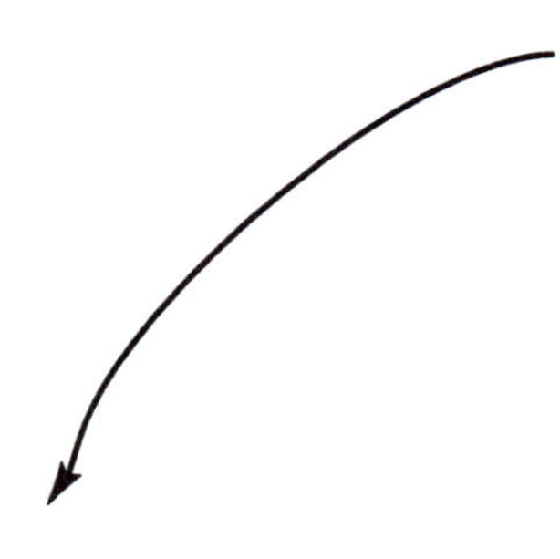

Tools

Paper
Pencil
pen
These are our tools
Don't be ashamed of such prudence.
Language has power
to pull ideas from the depths
to let our thoughts bloom
if only once in a lifetime
to make the sun rise again.

Writing a Vision

Darkness and light
primal, instinctive motions of the hands
keep a record of the night
a record of the light blooming in the free
of forgetting and remembering.
Tools of writing won't tear up the world,
rather shape it to your vision,
vision of the word,
vision of the sun rising again.
Bloom, unknowing forms,
write into the night.
Freedom,
freedom,
freedom in the dark.

Courage

Keep courage through your darkest moments.
It's necessary when you're slipping, sloping.
Don't cover your heart—it's not shameful.
The power of the word,
the flow of the voice,
the bloom of the feeling,
makes clear hearts rejoice and fly
like startled birds.
Hearts open and bloom not once
but many times, life times.
Pain is a prudent necessity.
The sun will rise after the night.

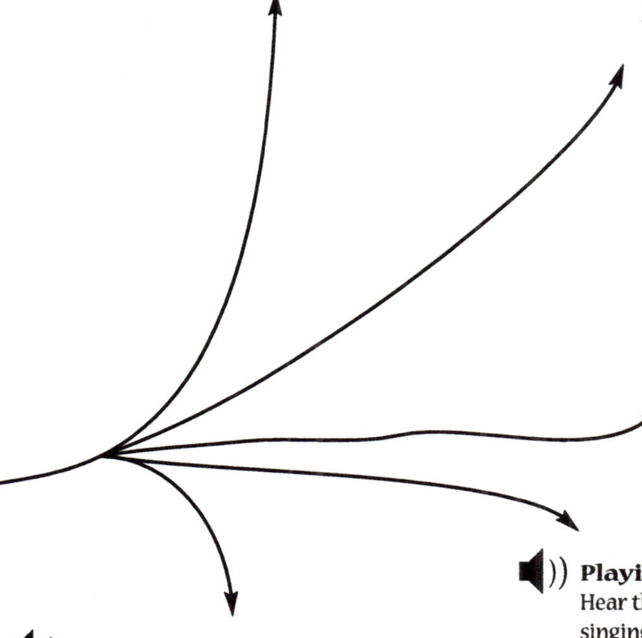

Do It Now

Write now,
right now,
chasing the ephemeral
chattering birds of midnight.
Help yourself to see the
fading visions of a once-blooming tree.
Trust your trails along the
grainy paper.
They will lead you
out of the darkness into the light,
right now, if you write now.

Playing in the Dark

Hear that tune
singing to itself in your head.
It may not stay like the fading memory
of a seventies hit. . .
but there is nothing shameful
in forgetting.
Feel how one hand presses the strings,
the other plucks,
aiding each other, working together,
pulling a song from the depths
of uncertainty.
It may be like a strangely-marked bird,
or an exotic flower that only lasts
one evening
but causes the sun to rise again.

Idea

These shapes I have made
are almost letters.
I can almost read them. And now,
I am sure there was a vision there
that was so clear, so pure
that its urgency was like the blooming
of a flower, the flight of a bird.
Now the sun has risen with its own
urgency,
and I can see now that there must have been
something more,
but I cannot remember exactly
what it was.

Expanding on the Process:

Inspired by the source, the melody that startles them into writing, re-creators approximate, adapt, modulate, permutate, transform, digress. The instability generated by surprise nudges listeners to re-group sounds, sense, and images, to unfold from the original into their own meaning, to vary, fluctuate, shuffle, connect this to that— in short, to open up their whole mind to the heard melody.

Re-creations illustrate the infinite, iterative number of possible human responses to a given art work, given word, or given act. We ourselves have many different voices in our heads. Each work of art can speak in many voices. That is the impact of a source. Many Re-creations will have some kind of echo of the original. But those echoes can reside in the words, in the sound, in the emotional, in narrative, in theme.

Not only are our minds are stretched by our own surprising and unique response, but—when shared (the subject of Chapter 10)—by seeing other responses of multiple voices to the same stimulus. We begin to see the multiple perspectives of a source, depending on whose unique experiential sieve it is filtered through.

There's a big difference between Re-creation and interpretation. Interpretation tends to close off other avenues, tending to zero in on the *right* interpretation, eliminating the diversity of the response. However, as art, any work of art will be dynamically unfinished, made whole only in the listener's mind. To make my point, let's look at two final poems, obliquely related because they are both about plums, which my students re-created in a diversity of responses, yet which sustain a connection with each original. What interested me about these poems and their Re-creations is that the first is about a *plum*; the second, about *the word plum*. These are subtle but decided differences, which are ultimately reflected in the way they are processed in the minds of their Re-creators:

The Plum
Nan Fry

Dark globe that fits easily into the palm,
your skin is speckled with pale galaxies,
an endless scattering.
Everywhere Adam and Eve are leaving
the Garden. You are the fruit we pluck
and eat. We need no serpent to urge us,
drawn as we are to your swelling,
your purple shading to rose, your skin
that yields to the touch, to the teeth:
all the world's waters and all it sweetness
rolled into fruit that explodes
on the tongue. We eat and drink flesh
the color of garnets, rubies, wounds.
It is bitter just under the skin.

Loss

Water, full and bitter, fills
the swelling rose.
Dark fruit rots in the wound
of garnet flesh.
The garden lies barren,
foliage scattered,
trees unyielding,
fruit uneaten.

The Plum

The plum— all water and sweetness,
a dark glove among the galaxies,
changing color from purple to rose
as precious as garnets and rubies.
The jeweled skins feels good to the touch
of fingers and teeth.
No serpent lured Adam and Eve
to this treasure,
the plum—bitter under the skin.

Food

It is not merely sustenance,
not merely the fuel that lights our energy.
Eating, when done well
(though not necessarily well-done)
is an orgy for the senses:
Colors explode and meld on a delicate plate
as ecstatic odors assail the nose,
encouraging the tongue to quiver,
salty saliva to flow.
Then, broken down and blended,
the delightful mush
slides delectably down the silken throat,
leaving room for more.

Ripe Fruit

The ripe fruit rests in my hand,
a microcosm of my entire existence.
Dark and forbidding, the
slick skin conceals the
richness of life-giving flesh beneath.
Life-sustaining, the proof of life
within the life of my hand.
I do not heed the encouragement of
original sin—I crush its life
under the force of my jaws.

Sweet Plum

The plum is garnished
in dark skin
yielding to the touch
waiting for teeth
We need no serpent
to warn us from its sweetness
the juices explode
as the speckled skin breaks
bitter under its skin
yet full of sweet juice
Adam and Eve tasted.
Oh, the sweet plum.

Eating the Plums

"Forgive me, for I have eaten
the plums you saved in the icebox,"
William Carlos Williams' poems
of love and life and the sweet desserts
of forbidden fruits.
What is in these bloody galaxies of bittersweet
juice and flesh and skin that is so tempting?
Can any man or woman eat these swelling
globes without feeling the pop of the "P" on one's lips
or the sweet thrumming of the "M" on one's tongue?
To hold so much sweetness in my hand
and bite fully, deeply, skin yielding
as I chew up and use this flesh to feed my own,
I feel part of a larger world of plum lovers
of those who suck life's juices boldly,
smacking our lips, raising our cups to the sun,
and laughing as we dance on the fruits
of many poets' labors.

Harvest

Temptation everywhere surrounds us,
thorns prick us when we rub and shake the tree for more.
Our appetite knows two tastes: bitter and sweet.
The fruit comes in different sizes,
our palate unknown to either until the color turns to tastes
tart sometimes
sweet, others.
With so much fruit around us, fruitfulness in us, on us—
speckles on our palms glowing and vibrant,
still, the bitter aftertaste lingers until we pluck out
the riper ones to satiate ourselves.

Loss

Katlin, you were like the plum, a garnet, a ruby,
pale-faced, hair like dusky fruit that shadowed your face.
Your body yielded to the galaxies.
We are left the skin of the fruit, an empty cradle,
small baskets of clothes. I touched you one last time,
watching you kick, reaching for a terrycloth butterfly.
You are a wound now, not a plum. Our hands are
empty, but your iridescence leaves a light in my heart.

The Plum evoked much more sinister stories of the archetypal danger of sweetness, the story of Adam and Eve, the inescapable presence of polarities in life, than the second poem below on, not just *Plum*, but *The Word Plum*, which gives an entirely new context to the subject of *plumness*. The subtle shift from the thing itself, the plum, to the name of it, the resonant sound/taste play, evident in *The WORD Plum*, is picked up by the listeners who, in their Re-creations, were nudged also to focus on the language aspect of *plum*—it's sounds, its syllables, its words in the mouth:

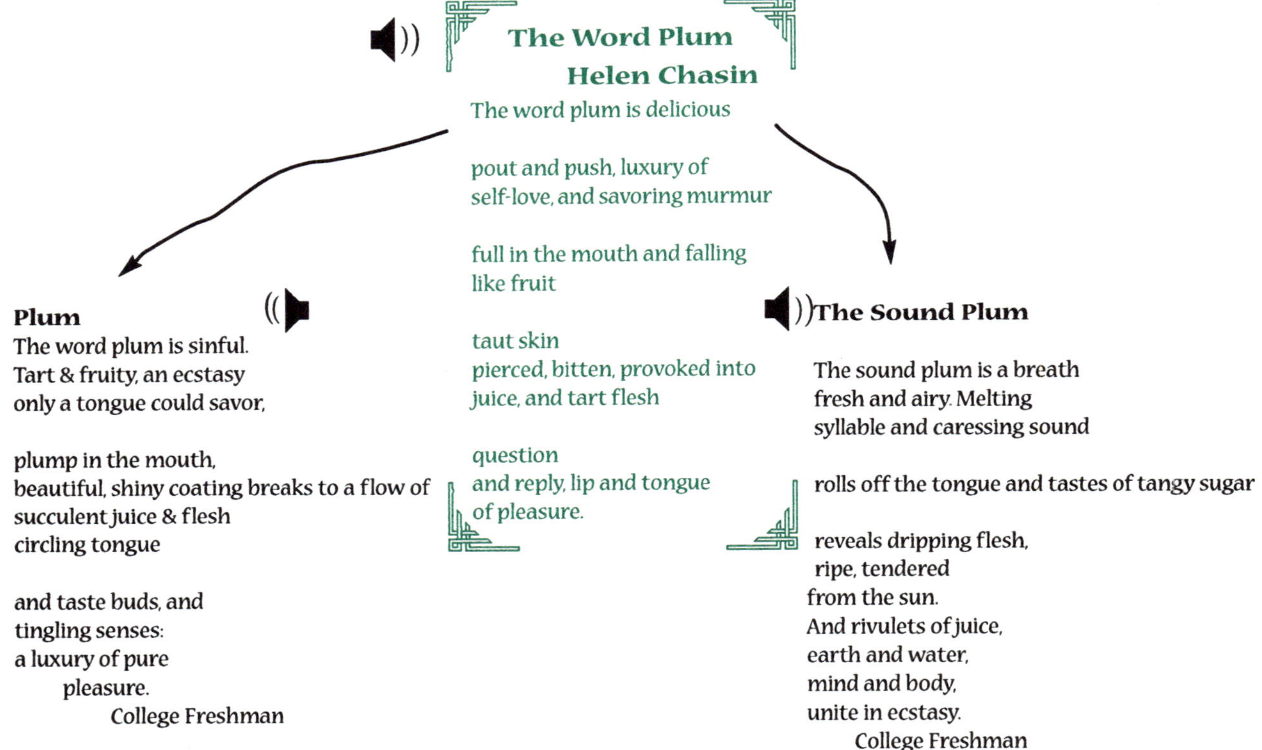

What We Can Learn from Learning about the Process of Re-creations:

In the two Re-creations above, the clear focus is on something once removed from the thing itself , PLUM, to focus on the sound *plum* or the word *plum*, as the poet of the original does. Each Re-creation of *The Plum* plays with sound or image much more than with a story about *the word plum*, as though the listeners knew this *story* is once removed from the *plum* itself. In exploring the process of Re-creations, I have come to the following conclusions: Anyone who is invited to re-create becomes an adaptor. The mental process of adaptation, according to biologist Konrad Lorenz, is "a dismantling of structures." He explains that "the gaining of new information demands the breaking down of some previous structure which, up to that moment, had appeared to be final" (1977). Similarly, the implication of the word *learn* implies an on-going restructuring of lived-through experience, resulting in a continual dismantling, modifying, synthesizing, then restructuring, and finally, reintegrating of the thing to be learned into a new synthesis. If learning does not build the experiential, the participatory, or the creative experience of the learner, the learning is shallow, transitory, and readily forgotten. Re-creations become the model of a creative spark which makes anyone experiencing it aware of the spark itself, of becoming aware of options, of the process of flexibility itself. Experiencing the process itself makes it immediate, makes each of us more aware of our own creative potential, makes it utilizable, teachable, learnable, even when we believe we have zero creative juice. The result startles us into a creative moment.

In hearing the language of a poem in sound, uttered by the human voice, we are asked to slow down, to listen, really listen, to focus on our mind as it pulls out bits of meaning from the images, the word rhythms, the images, the allusions, the descriptions, all of whose functions create a kind of coherence as their combinations create a new context in our minds. Hearing an already-created piece creates an imaginative as well as an emotional context. The heard piece thus provides the background in which a Re-creation can take place.

> Re-creations are a generative process, making connections, reorganizing existing patterns, and it all creates enormous energy.
>
> —Student

At its best, learning, reading/viewing/ interpreting is a dynamic process in which the reader/ viewer affects the thing being learned, read, viewed, interpreted. In such a learning world, everyone can be a participant or a creator, not primarily a passive observer. In this world, learning becomes active and in-volving so that not only are the images and words of creators palpable but but of the learners as well, in turn making palpable what they are learning and how they are learning it.

> In re-creating we only have time to spill our personal connections out on paper. There's no time to get scared.
>
> —Student

> We leap to correct answers before there are sufficient data, we intuit, we grasp, we jump to conclusions despite the lack of convincing evidence. That we are right more often than wrong is the miracle of human intellect.
>
> —Donald Norman, psychologist

> Poems are like dreams; in them you put what you don't know you know.
>
> —Adrienne Rich

> The poem is a momentary stay against confusion."
>
> —Robert Frost

C·H·A·P·T·E·R·T·W·O

Improvisation and Surprise

THE IMMEDIACY OF INVOLVEMENT

> Improvisation, writing, painting, invention—all creative acts are forms of play, the starting place of creativity in the human growth cycle, and one of the great primal life functions.
>
> —S. Nachmanovitch

The Surprise in Improvisation

> In painting, as in life, you must act directly. Picasso, 1935

Improvisation embodies the turbulence of life itself. The improvisational nature of Re-creations evoke, invite, facilitate the listener's involvement. This involvement cannot be forced by sequential steps; if we try, we kill the delicate resonance between listening/doing before it can unfold. Improvisation is a discovery process. When we improvise we become experimenters in the dance of life.

Improvisation operates at lightning speed adapting, changing, revising, communicating, connecting, disconnecting, reconnecting, playing with the initial impulses, triggering the discovery of meaning. The improvisational moment invites us to be present in the moment, alert to noticing.

> In quickness is truth... the only style worth tiger-trapping.
>
> —Ray Bradbury

Improvisation. The word is familiar, but few of us have a clear idea of what it means. We associate it with jazz, yet improvisation is part of our lives. Yet most of us have little idea what happens when we do it or how to engage it consciously. I certainly didn't.

Improvisation means to compose and perform or deliver without previous preparation; to do something on spur of the moment; to make, provide, or arrange from whatever materials are readily available. The word comes from the Latin *im* + *provisus* = pp of *providere* to see beforehand; unpremeditated, unrehearsed, unprepared.

> Intuition is quick, immediate, and ambiguous. Logic is sequential, careful, and deliberate.
>
> —Percy Bysshe Shelley

As children, we improvise constantly as a way of learning. The purpose of improvisation is the experimental unfolding of patterns. It is transformative, modifying, a playful extension of available knowledge to novel *phenomena.* For example, James Britton (1970) describes his two- and one-half-year old daughter's first encounter with strawberries: Holding them, she observed: "They are like cherries." She tasted them and said, "They are just like sweeties (candies)." Then, "they are like red ladybirds." Improvising on what she already knew, she connected experiences of redness, sweetness, roundness, spottedness which she had encountered with cherries, sweeties, ladybirds.

> What might be taken for a precocious genius is the genius of childhood. When the child grows up, it disappears without a trace. It may happen that this boy will become a real painter some day, or even a great painter. But then he will have to begin everything again, from zero.
>
> — Picasso (in Brassai, 1966)

The Empty Circle: Inverse Clustering

One way to become conscious of our improvisational gifts is to find a way to catch our fleeting associations. Clustering words and phrases from a heard source--around an empty circle--is a bid to receptivity, an internal permit to let improvisation happen. It is a way of lighting a match of creativity instead of having to wait for lightning to strike. Clustering around an empty center turns out to be a fundamental search strategy, a prospecting of the field, an exploration of the moment.

The lightning speed of our associational right hemisphere is easily derailed by the more systematic left hemisphere which censors or judges. Inverse clustering around a blank circle is a way of destabilizing habitual thought. It allows discrete words or phrases come together on the page- - the beginning of a new pattern. Some of these words are amplified through feelings or perceptions which lead to the sense of a vague whole, a partial melody, a relatedness. This sense of connection triggers expression.

Here is where SURPRISE comes in. Almost always, when we engage in such improvisational play, we are startled into an emotional jolt. The surprise in improvisation is an example of simultaneous continuity and discontinuity. The very disorientation pushes the mind into sporadic, intermittent leaps, skipping between feelings, among thoughts, resulting in a new convergence. We re-create in our own way. We can't copy because the words are not fixed on a page before us. We can't cheat because there are no set answers. We can only let the impact of artifact and self-generated images collide. This collision, surprise, shock, discomfort, produces a personal response, not just a knee-jerk *reaction* to the heard piece that allows us to ride on the energy of the already- created pattern we are hearing. The mind takes in and reshapes it into its own pattern of meaning.

Words are saturated with shades of meaning, and since we are given permission to be plunged into uncertainty, the Re-creation self-evolves through a kind of combinatory play (Nachmanovitch, Johnston, Einstein). In inverse clustering, the brain deconstructs the heard whole into a few words and phrases which do not as yet have a center, a focus, a theme. With the naming of the center, a tentative focus swims into mental view. The previously random words and phrases around the blank center are attracted—like iron filings to a magnet—by the naming, resulting in a ferment of writing.

A semblance to the original is not necessary, although it can be. Since the two and one-half minute Re-creation is nothing more than a first, raw, very raw draft, no one needs to worry about direction, about using too many of the original words, or about identity. The Re-creation has a connection to the source, but it becomes its own piece in the process of transforming the original. Let's look at a manifesto about writing in the following poem:

Ars Poetica
Vicente Huidobro

Let poetry be like a key
Opening a thousand doors.
A leaf falls; something flies by;
Let all the eye sees be created
And the soul of the listener tremble.

Invent new worlds and watch your word;
The adjective, when it doesn't give life, kills it.

We are in the age of nerves.
The muscle hangs,
Like a memory, in museums;
But we are not the weaker for it:
True vigor
Resides in the head.

Oh Poets, why sing of roses!
Let them flower in your poems;

For us alone
Do all things live beneath the Sun.

The poet is a little God

Scribing Words
We scribe our words on blank pages
creating roses where none existed before.
We are the creators, the gods of verse.
The rose will bloom,
the petals fall,
swirling in the wind of our imagination
glistening in the morning sun
quieting the nerves
relaxing the muscles,
a door to our souls,
each one different.

Stuck
As nerves fray,
ideas flower in the
early hours of dawn and
God looks on and laughs
as a 1000 doors open
and we are too tired to write,
and out of coffee.
The sun rises
and a bird flies past your world,
and you only wish you had the key
to make this happen at 5 P.M.

Keys
There is a key to the world.
The key falls
and leaves us to invent our own.
Key words are killed off.
We are rich and full
of energy of mind.
We have the memory
making of us poets.

Unlock the Door
Watch the word
and listen to the smells
of roses that bloom
from poems.
Let your soul tremble toward
the sun with outstretched muscles
and nerves.
Unlock the door to museums of memory
and temples of gods.
Remove the lock;
throw away the key.

Life Artist
The journey you take:
find a way to share it
and, with your story,
let the soul of the listener tremble.
Be an inspiration.
Do not sing of roses.
Let them flower on their own.
Do not mimic. Rather, create.
Live a limitless life.

Comment:

I have found that the process of Re-creation is the most organic creative, cooperative act between between artifact and listener. Re-creation nudges the hearer to become more than just a *spectator*, so to speak, but a true participant in the creative act. I am after shifts, departures from the original, veering into one's own mental or emotional territory, straying from the original to be shocked into surprise.

Two

Two trains roar toward each other,
pass, and all is silent.
The grass by the tracks
is both short and tall.

Needs

She needs a husband
he wants a wife
they think they have common tastes goals and dreams
they think they love each other
they say they love each other
they grow to be like each other
but when she realizes
that needing a husband
is not what she needs
their tastes goals dreams
and love
are no longer common

Marriage

two people, alike, different,
independent, dependent,
agreeing, disagreeing,
leaving the door at least ajar
Yes, that is the secret--
always leaving the door at least ajar.

Simple Song

Marge Piercy

When we are going toward someone we say
You are just like me
your thoughts are my brothers
word matches word
how easy to be together.

When we are leaving someone we say:
how strange you are
we cannot communicate
we can never agree
how hard, hard and weary to be together.

We are not different nor alike
but each strange in his leather body
sealed in skin and reaching out clumsy
hands
and loving is an act
that cannot outlive
the open hand
the open eye
the door in the chest standing open.

You and I

We can never be truly together
you and me
though we shift, forward
and back
journeying through life,
leading to death, to strangeness.

How can we love, when we
don't know who we are?
Who are you to me:
the same,
different?
I say,'I love you' now, when we
come together.
What will I say when we
grow apart?

Differences

A simple song of differences:
How you cock your head
in that funny way;
how your little toes
each crookedly reach out
to separate destinations;
how your silly smile
tells me
I am different, too.

We

When we agree
I like you
we are one
a team.
When we disagree
I don't like you
we are separate
you are my enemy.
Human nature is strange.
We all have leather skin,
we are all clumsy,
we all need love.
So, open your hand
and the chest will open with treasures.

What We are

We are so different,
you and I,
noticeable only at a distance.
Walking closer we become one
divisible by two,
so much alike we know
and think in unison, as if
a door were opened,
and we could walk in
and see the life each holds.

We are so much alike
you and I,
noticeable only
at close range,
man and woman
flesh and hair and bone
and heart and soul.

The Black Snake

Mary Oliver

When the black snake
flashed onto the morning road,
and the truck could not swerve—
death, that is how it happens.

Now he lies looped and useless
as an old bicycle tire.
I stop the car
and carry him into the bushes.

He is as cool and gleaming
as a braided whip, he is as beautiful and quiet
as a dead brother.
I leave him under the leaves

and drive on, thinking
about death: its suddenness,
its terrible weight,
its certain coming. Yet under

reason burns a brighter fire, which the bones
have always preferred.
It is the story of endless good fortune.
It says to oblivion: not me!

It is the light at the center of every cell.
It is what sent the snake coiling and flowing forward
happily all spring through the green leaves before
he came to the road.

Snake

The snake, compelled by life,
meets his death on the road.
Death: sudden, heavy, certain.
Life: light, energy, forward-propelling
moves us all toward
the end of the road.

Forward

The snake, straight, forward, into the road,
the never always into the ocean, always straight
forward, and in the end, curving around, coiling,
a unity, beginning to end and back again, this
snake, instinct pushing, pulling it forward,
knowing, not knowing. Straight forward still, to
die, to touch me, to add fuel to the fire inside
of me. Not me, I say. Not me, I announce. The
snake shows it differently. You, says the snake,
you and me. Bending down, I touch the snake,
the whip, the straight coiled line, the never. I stand
in the road, life, olive, the fire still believing in
my bones, the life still pushing me forward,
straight ahead. Straight and forward, into life,
into death, again and always forward into
the road.

What's Scary

Who wants to think of death?
My mind rejects the snake's story.
It may be closer to home than I can deal with.
Death happens, but that is no consolation to me.
It's not always sudden.
Sometimes you know well in advance.
That's the scary part.

Snuffed

Appeared like lightning,
snuffed like a match.
Black snake crushed
on black pavement,
looped and braided
like heavy chains.

Comment: Without previous discussion of the poem the students heard, their Re-creations, written in less than three minutes, demonstrate a depth of understanding: the snake is not some alien creature. They grasp that we are the snake, moving through life until some terrible accident—or non-accident overtakes us. They know at some level-- even if they reject it-- that the death, of accident, of possible—and likely—unpredictable endings of our lives are a *terrible weight*: They can infer their own endings; they can imagine their future.

It's Not That Bad

It could be worse:
Nothing could be simmering on the stove.
Four kids could be running unsupervised through the house.
The Mexican catholic nanny could be confessing
she's pregnant and wants an abortion.
Your wife could be having an affair with your best friend,
and the white bone china could be
in pieces on the dining room floor.

Alone

Peeling off his clothes.
Just like the skin of
the tangerine,
the peeling is bitter.
He plunges into the cold bay naked.
He shrivels up like the fall sun
settling quickly into darkness.
There is no one home; the house is empty.
Surrounding him are oaks, thick, impersonal, and tall.

Homecoming

I am the Soul's thrown
white Body, empty
as a naked Bone
lying yellow in
my own heat.

Song

Robert Hass

Afternoon cooking in the fall sun—
who is more naked
than the man
yelling, "Hey, I'm home!"
to an empty house?
thinking because the bay is clear,
the hills in yellow heat,
& scrub oak red in gullies
that great crowds of family
should tumble from the rooms
to throw their bodies on the Papa-body
I-am-loved.

Cat sleeps in the windowgleam,
dust motes.
On the oak table
filets of sole
stewing in the juice of tangerines,
slices of green pepper
on a bone-white dish.

Soles or Souls?

The heat of the afternoon cooking my soles,
I scream, naked, in an empty house
for other bodies to press against my Papa-Bear body.
The sleeping cat eyes me
through swirling dust motes with contempt.
I am a blank stare
of flavors that just don't mix
and are always separate if somewhat entangled.

Out, Out, Damn Spot

Gift me not your presence here,
Darken not my door.
Take your body elsewhere.
Dirty not my floor.

What we had was long ago.
What we have is now.
So shall I have my freedom,
And you shall have to go.

Call Me

Who is more naked than the woman
who says, 'Call me.'
She will wait in an empty house
with crowded space and think
of tumbling bodies
in the bone-white bedroom.
Dust will settle in her mind
when it's over,
and when some new man
swishes his spinach
over an ivory plate,
she will be naked again,
clothed in nothing more than hope.

Still Life

It is a perfect still-life of a homecoming. Framed in gold and white, the afternoon seems perfect in its gilded cloak. An orange cat complements the scene, never stirring, just being. Only the jarring entrance of a needy, shouting human who doesn't appreciate the beauty of the scene, breaks the mood. The still-life shatters. Now it is just a stage, waiting to be invaded by this arrogant thespian whose expectations must be met. The cat never stirs, but knows in its dream-world that humans can never be trained. They do not earn peace, and they are unworthy of such beauty. The cat purrs on, dreaming of the filet of sole, ignoring the interruption. The man will go away. But for a cat, there are endless such afternoons, afternoons of gold and quiet where a nearly-perfect animal can be part of a still-life, a work of art, a treasure.

The Magic of Early Fall

The late summer, early fall waves on Oahu are best. As a kid I remember enjoying myself like no other time. The sky seemed somehow even clearer and, if possible, more blue. The waves were the last of the summer swells to arrive along Oahu's south shore. The guys in the water all seemed to appreciate this fact, especially since all the kids were back in school. If the swell was good enough, all the things you'd ever heard about the individual surf spots came true. Ala Moana lined up out at the buoy and threw out a tube far enough down the trough to dance in. Speed was essential, for the end was a ride across the wave, face in the shallow and dreaded bowl area. God, what electricity, what a thrill to be part of such dynamic natural forces. I forget who I am. Those late summer, early fall waves still break in my heart.

Comment: I am after tapping into the marvelous instability that characterizes the creative human mind, leading to fluctuation, variation; I am after the hunches, guesses, surprising configurations that take shape, as in the last Re-creation, *It's Not That Bad,* in which the writer was *goofing off* in spinning his version of the story, but, at the same time, we can see that he was genuinely listening. I am after connecting the created artifact with the personal. I want the created artifact to hover, hang fire, hum, in the listening mind, tapping into the global feelings, into the human need to create patterns of meaning, into understanding at the deepest level, no matter how far-ranging.

Why Poems as Source for Inspiration?

> Poetry is the place where thinking and feeling become one.
> —O. Paz

A poem is a compressed whole, a fusion of seeing and believing. Although a poem uses ordinary language, it tells us things quite out of the ordinary. The students whose Re-creations we are reading in these pages and hearing on the CD span the spectrum of age and majors. Most of the students here are freshmen and sophomores in college; there are a few graduate students and some adults. Most of them are engineering students or business degree students, and the full range between. The bottom line is that rarely, if ever, have these students willingly read poetry. Yet, in each of their Re-creations, irrespective of age or skill in writing, we can distinguish four characteristics:

- Emotional involvement;
- Discovery of a pattern which they are able to express;
- Improvisational skills;
- Ability to read between the lines to get to the essence of something despite lack of training.

Re-creations get at human experience, the intuitive, the holistic, the emotional, which is not easily verbalizable. British scientist Michael Polanyi wrote,"We know more than we can tell"—that is, literally more than we can. Knowing is not just logical. For as long as human beings have been curious about how we know and learn, different ages have recognized the distinction between the sequential nature of logic and the patterning, holistic nature of images. This distinction underlies many of the polarities we encounter in the history of culture: Apollonian (with its emphasis on reason and control)/Dionysian (with its welling up of image and feeling); part/whole; atomistic/holistic; logical/metaphorical; left/right; sign/design. Ingmar Bergman tellingly focused on one key difference between these two ways of knowing:

> I throw a spear into the dark--that is intuition.
> Then I have to send an expedition into
> the jungle to find the way of the spear—
> that is logic.

And there we have it in a nutshell: Spear/intuition is quick, immediate, ambiguous—half a line. The second is sequential, deliberate, and step-by-step—exploratory. What is most important to understand here is that both ways are integral to human knowing and human expression. Clearly, both logical comprehension and image/feeling apprehension are fundamental to the way the human mind works. One is implicit; the other explicit. These Re-creations tap into the holistic, intuitive, quick, immediate, improvisational only to open the channels to expression which must incorporate sequence, logic, syntax. The process enables—rather than disables—the complementary functions of the two modes of knowing available to us.

> When we are kids we make up things, we write, and for me the puzzle is not that some people are still writing. the real question is why did the other people stop?
> —William Stafford

The creative process needs both implicit and explicit, intuition and logic, image and sequence. Moving back and forth, these small, ongoing shifts between these two modes of knowing lead to destabilization of habitual thinking, finally producing a greater shift in growth. As listeners jot down words and phrases, their thoughts leap with lightning speed from this to that, all within the newer context of *both/and* instead of *either/or*. This realization is important, for our culture wrongly teaches us that thoughts and feelings lie in almost separate worlds. In fact, they're always intertwined, oscillating back and forth between not-knowing and knowing, understanding and not-understanding, between losing our way and finding our way, between intuition and logic, between confusion and discovery. The Re-creations on these pages let us see the absolute necessity of the dynamic interplay between these two impulses, between these two ways of knowing. Novelist Henry James used the telling image of a pair of scissors to remind us that this complementarity of the human mind—like scissors,neither one of which can cut in the absence of the other blade—needs to be activated, used, developed. One without the other is useless.

> Like every beginner, I thought you could beat, pummel, and thrash an idea into existence. Under such treatment of course, any decent idea folds up its paws, fixes its eyes on eternity, and dies.
> Ray Bradbury

> The challenge of re-creating is simultaneously in the act of risking and of trust. Both helped me to write my re-creation.
> — Student

> In my group the most powerful re-creations—I think—were those generated by strong personal feeling .
> —Student

What We Can Learn:

We learn from the examples of Re-creations in this book and research in many domains of knowledge that meaning-making is ultimately an improvisational, indeterminate process with random variables which cannot be eradicated. Let us make use of that uncertainty. Wherever the heard original leads us in the moment—far afield, close to home, somewhere in the middle of the field-- when the time comes for looking at any piece critically, that is the time is to re-write, to re-phrase, to re-combine, any chunks of the original which are too derivative, too pat. The original is only the diving board from which to launch. The dive into improvisation is the key to discovering direction. When listening is a genuine goal, there is no *right* answer for which one can aim, as poet Jared Carter describes so tellingly in his villanelle:

Improvisation

Jared Carter

To improvise, first let your fingers stray
across the keys like travelers in snow:
each time you start, expect to lose your way.

You'll find no staff to lean on, none to play
among the drifts the wind has left in rows.
To improvise, first let your fingers stray

beyond the path. Give up the need to say
which way is right, or what the dark stones show;
each time you start, expect to lose your way.

And what the stillness keeps, do not betray;
the one who listens is the one who knows.
To improvise, first let your fingers stray;

out over emptiness is where things weigh
the least. Go there, believe a current flows
each time you start: expect to lose your way.

Risk is the pilgrimage that cannot stay;
the keys grow silent in their smooth repose.
To improvise, first let your fingers stray.
Each time you start, expect to lose your way.

CHAPTER THREE

Listening

HEARING THE MELODY BEFORE THE NOTES

Listening is different from hearing. We can *hear* talk emanating from a room full of people, but we may not be *listening*. We hear the radio or the TV in the background, but we are not necessarily listening. We hear ourselves read aloud, but we may not know what we are reading. Biologist R. W. Gerard tells of a small boy who was reading aloud. When asked about the meaning of what he had read, said, "I don't know. I wasn't listening." (1952) Hearing is passive; listening is active. In order to learn, we have to do more than just hear; we learn to listen.

Reading Text and Listening to Text:

When we listen to a text, we listen to the whole which is more than the sum of its parts—of sound, emotions, words. Words in turn evoke mental images which activate brain centers that allows us to have virtual experience. When we listen, our minds ask questions as we scan the whole in an effort to understand. If the words don't *go together*, or if the idea expressed is sketchy, the mind skillfully fills in the missing links, creating a new frame of reference, such as Richard Ressman's *Photography* vignette.

Listening is not only the most important sense for understanding speech, it becomes a kind of oral shorthand for emerging patterns of meaning that are not necessarily communicated in the silence of print. Leonard Shlain, author of *The Alphabet and the Goddess*, argues that "speech is the consummate act of improvisation and everyone, at one time or another, has been surprised by her or his own eloquence. He reminds us that speech generation and listener comprehension are simultaneous events, framed in the here and now, whereas the context of writing is there and then." What is missing from the written word, according to Shlain is "the aesthetic quality of the speaker's voice," evoking different emotional responses: "While consciously attending to the content of spoken language, the listener is also evaluating speech's emotional tenor subliminally." Thus, he concludes that speech depends more on a "bicameral cooperative effort" between the hemispheres. The tone of voice and the choice of words carry information that allows us to hear between the lines and sequences of spoken language.

Linguist Steven Pinker refers to human language as the "epitome of flexible behavior." Explaining that language understanding proceeds from raw sound up through representations of syllables, words and phrases, to an understanding of the content of the message, he says that, "in the sound wave arriving at our ears, syllables and words are warped and smeared together" so that what we hear is not a sequence but a pattern of meaning. This pattern of meaning is constructed from many clues, such as tonality, inflection, and rhythm that that are crucial components of speech. Pinker reminds us that "a change in the enunciation and emphasis of certain phrases and words can subtly redirect the entire meaning of a message." Listening to a poem pulls us into the aesthetic quality of the human voice, evoking different emotional responses, affected by the emotional tenor of what is heard.

Sound and Silence:

When we really listen, we hear both sound and silence. The patterns of sounds as well as the silences between them enables us to listen to the melody of something heard. In silence, our two hemispheres have a chance to communicate, have a moment to connect, to intuit, for possible insight, inspiration. Most of the time we don't know it, but insight comes of its own accord. But we have to listen in active quiescence.

For active quiescence to take hold, listening is necessary. The active quiescence leads to awareness of melody, which in turn leads to naming a melody in words, which leads to the silence of writing following listening, the absorption of the melody resonating in the listener's head. Re-creators, at that moment, forget there are other people in the room, who are also writing. Active quiescence takes us into an eye, into a vortex of energy. To be actively present and quiescent at the same time, we slow down, breathe. In this state, sound and silence are in relationship to one another, not opposites. In such silence one's own melody can emerge. Alice Brand and Richard Graves insist that "silence is the first teacher of writing, and it is everywhere throughout the process."

Inverse clustering:

In inverse clustering, the center is not named first but last, just before the writing occurs. The process of jotting down words and phrases nudges the hearer into being a listener, allows thoughts to bunch, group, cluster. Out of this jostling agglomeration of images, ideas, and analogous leaps from an unfamiliar piece listened to, a focus swims into view. From the swarming, transient crowds of associations as we listen, the pull of a melody—likely emotional—becomes a strange attractor, tugging at the mind's attention in this direction or that. The seemingly random words and phrases around the blank center are like random iron filings cast on a surface. As soon as that blank circle is named, the very naming becomes a magnet for the filings as they begin organize themselves in spectacular patterns around that center. At this point the listening bears fruit and a Re-creation can be written in minutes.

Orality and Print:

That is where the sound of the human voice comes in. The kind of listening resulting in active quiescence can rarely happen in print, especially for most students. Hearing print read well, especially the patterns of poetry, pushes us into the active quiescence that makes listening possible. When we listen to a pattern of meaning—a poem, for instance—as opposed to *reading it*—we listen differently. This difference enables us to reach a state of active quiescence.

In a state of active quiescence, we are totally receptive, open to what enters our ears, our mind, our emotions. Listening, we discover webs of relationships. Artificial intelligence guru, Roger Shank, says that listening is essential to creative behavior because we can store ideas and images only when we are really attending, which means simultaneously sorting, discarding, and keeping. In the process of Re-creations, the mind is surprised into attending. "The creative mind needs data from which to work," he says.

Listening to the resonant voice of a poem differs from reading. Active listening automatically lets us consolidate a number of mental skills, including emotional processing, including the emergence of intention. In listening to something to be re-created, we already know we are going to DO something with what we've heard without the pressure of the *right* answer. We listen. We enjoy. We associate. We re-create—but in our own way. We can't memorize what we've just heard; it moves too fast. We can't copy; the words are not fixed on a page before us. We can't cheat; there are no set answers. We can only let the heard piece and images it generates in our minds collide.

This collision—resulting in recognition, wondering, shock, discomfort, or surprise—produces a personal response. We actually ride on the energy of the already created artifact in order to produce something that is OURS.

Narrow and Wide Attention (High Focus/Low Focus):

Listening has to do with the ability to reconstruct mentally what we're hearing into our own ever-shifting internal knowledge map. Ironically, listening has more to do with wide attention instead of narrow attention. Wide attention is subtly reciprocal with the resonant voice. When we listen with wide attention instead of with a narrow focus, we are reading between the words, so to speak, for what the whole tells us. Not only do we listen to what the poem is about, we also listen to what the poem is *not* about—and, analogously, to what we are about, as well.

To understand why and how Re-creations produce such stunning results, let's look at the mental process involved. In listening to something read, such as a poem—already a pattern in itself—we shift from our more common *narrow attention to detail* to *wide attention* to the whole (Joanna Field). Computer scientist David Gelernter calls narrow attention *high focus* and wide attention, *low focus*. Narrow attention is clearly focused, wide attention, diffuse.

> Like a woman with a flashlight I can throw the bright circle of my awareness where I choose....The beam of my attention is not of fixed width, I can widen or narrow its focus as I choose: wide and narrow attention: only a tiny act of will is necessary in order to pass from one to the other.
>
> —Joanna Field 1937

In our dual minds, the left hemisphere's ability to sequence details leads to high focus. When narrow purposes are held in check, the right hemisphere's wide attention (low focus) clicks in, making it possible to look at the big picture. *High focus*, according to Gelernter, is "goal-oriented and automatic for everyday affairs, selecting what serves its immediate interests, ignoring the rest. Low focus is diffuse, fluidic, taking in the whole rather than its parts when there is no immediate given problem, no search for a single solution." Many researchers have noticed these two ways of knowing, attending, focusing (not to mention poets and artists over many centuries):

The Bright Circle of Awareness: Two Modes of Attention	
Right Hemisphere	Left Hemisphere
Wide Attention	Narrow Attention (Joanna Field)
Low Focus	High Focus(David Gelernter)
Presentational	Discursive (Susanne Langer)
Ampliative	Explicative (C. S. Peirce)
Tacit	Explicit (M. Polanyi)
Metaphoric	Rational (Jerome Bruner)
Appositional	Propositional (Joseph Bogen)
Design Mind	Sign Mind (Gabriele Rico)
Implicit	Explicit (Renee Fuller)
Lateral	Vertical (Edward de Bono)
Multiple	Sequential (Ulric Neisser)
Diffuse	Focused (Polanyi, 1955)
Infinite	Finite (James Carse)
Reflexive	Extensive (Janet Emig)
Allatonce	One-at-a-time

In the first column, the mental strategies named describe the search for a *big picture*, interlaced with affect, with no single goal in mind. In the second column, the mental strategies named all reduce the beam of attention to a specific issue, instance, goal. So the bright circle of human awareness shifts according to how we process incoming information, shifts according to our intent.

These designations are nothing new. In 1911 William James wrote about the value of both wide and narrow attention that "...for some purposes the one, for other purposes the other, has the higher value. Who can decide offhand which is absolutely better.... We must do both alternately, and a human [should] not limit himself to either any more than a pair of scissors can cut with a single one of its blades."

The human mind, through its wide and narrow modes of attention, is so flexibly designed as to accommodate the ambiguous, the paradoxical, the fuzzy, the uncertain, and to *re-cognize* it (to know it again) as a pattern of meaning. From the Latin *recognoscere*, to know again, it literally means a second knowing, a knowing again, usually without conscious awareness that something has been met before, only that it has a context that rings a bell somehow. Creative geniuses are likely to be outstanding at shuttling between wide and narrow attention.

Neurosurgeon Joseph Bogen speculates that the corpus callosum plays no small role in creative acts because it functions not only to transfer high-level information from one hemisphere to another but to inhibit it when only wide or only narrow attention is important for the moment. Bogen further speculates that creative surprise (the AHA! insight, illumination) happens at the instant when the two hemispheres momentarily lose their partial independence. In short, something clicks as the two interact in an unaccustomed way.

Re-creations foster that momentary interaction between wide and narrow attention which tends to result in creative surprise. Since a creative surprise, the shock of recognition, cannot be willed, we need a trigger, just as we need matches to produce a flame. Wide attention in listening to an already-created whole—the poem—is a way to jump-start the process. Listening, we begin with low focus, click into surprise, and probably end in high focus as our piece is finished on the page.

Knowing in advance that we will also DO something with our listening moments afterwards may engender mild anxiety. But when we are also told there are no rules about *how* to re-create—that, in fact, we can go in any direction our feelings, images, thoughts take us—there is a shift in the quality of our attention. We simply listen, widely, purely, watching our minds listening. During the second listening, we DO something with that listening, which is simply to *gather* words, images, phrases from what we are hearing—without a goal. This *gathering* takes place around a circle deliberately left blank. With completion of the second reading, the gathering is complete. Just so. Almost in an altered state of consciousness—and in less than three minutes—the mind and hand re-create the heard piece. The following original poems you will hear read on the CD become *triggers* for two and one-half minute Re-creations, most of them by college students. They are melodies in themselves, yet they vary from another in sound, in content, in voice, in direction.

Comment: Several Re-creations of Ciardi's short poem echo his rhythms: short, staccato lines, one and two-syllable words; most of them pick up Ciardi's focus of hurrying through life instead of stopping here and there to smell the roses. *Clockwork* is the one that explores at what was not directly in the poem—the pause that is a form of running.

The Sounds and Silences of Words:

Words matter. When we really listen, we begin to see how one word echoes or interacts with another word in a whole.

In the next poem by Octavio Paz, the whole turns on three words: stone/wind/ water. Re-creators went in different directions as they zeroed in on their own unique melody:

Wind and Water, and Stone
Octavio Paz

The water hollowed the stone,
the wind disperesed the water,
the stone stopped the wind.
Water and wind and stone.

The wind sculpted the stone,
the stone is a cup of water,
the water runs off and is winds.
Stone and wind and water.

The wind sings in it turning,
the water murmurs as it goes,
the motionless stone is quiet.
Wind and water and stone.

One is the other, and is neighter:
among their empty names
they pass and disappear,
water and stone and wind.

Circles

I hear an echo—deep
deep down, of the wind,
wind, wind—wind to water
water to stone
stone in water—thrown.
Rings circling in a pond of water
circling, circling
then still
I hear the echo
the song, the murmur, the stillness…
I have and am and maybe yet
shall come
full circle.

Rock, Paper, Scissors

Paper wraps Rock,
Rock smashes Scissors, Scissors cut Paper.
Ro-Sham-Bo
like picking numbers, only more fun.
Make a fist to smash the 'V'
of middle finger and index.
Spread out five fingers
to wrap a fist.
Form a 'V'
to cut the fingers.
If only life were so simple.

How to Name a Child

The name should be hollow,
able to hold the new-born dream.
It should be sculpted,
the shape of the infant itself
and the shape into which he will grow.
It should sing like the wind,
have turnings like water,
be solid and strong like stone.
It should be at once like an empty cup
and the quiet soft water that fills it.
Then, only then,
will the name disappear
and become the child.

Comment: The attractor of the original lies in the power of individual words: stone, water, wind. Yet each Listener transforms this focus into a personal pattern of meaning. We listen, imagine, remember, hypothesize, or ideate in order to understand for ourselves.

In Gwendolyn Brooks' poem, the words of the "hunchback girl," reflected in her voice speaking, impinge on the listener's ear to such an extent that virtually all of the Re-creations were in the first person.

Hunchback Girl: She Thinks of Heaven
Gwendolyn Brooks

My Father, it is surely a blue place
And straight. Right. Regular. Where I shall find
No need for scholarly nonchalance or looks
A little to the left or guards upon the
Heart to halt love that runs without crookedness
Along its crooked corridors. My Father,
It is a planned place surely. Out of coils,
Unscrewed, released, no more to be marvelous,
I shall walk straightly through most proper halls
Proper myself, princess of properness.

Conversation with My Dad
Father,
I wish I knew you
for myself—
I want to be selfish here, I want
you for me here, right now—
I was four when you left,
five when you died.
I cried, watched my family,
so scattered.
I remember
your face, father, even better
than Mom's—I have you all to myself
in my mind's eye, my imagination
where we talk and play freely—
even today.

Choosing
I am coming to you.
Do not turn your eyes,
do not guard your heart,
I have guarded my heart too long.
Straightly I look to you,
uncoiled, uncrooked,
not left, not right:
My Princess' gaze
chooses your blue eyes,
chooses you.

What I Am Not
It is a straight place
that coils between
blue and green, marvelous
colors, if you ask me.
They are nonchalant in their attention,
proper in their Princes' planned places.
But me,
I know
I am not blue nor green
I am not evening nor night,
not a rusted nickel,
not worth picking up from a subway grating,
am not inching to the left
nor to the right
nor forward nor back
but grounded of my own accord,
dressed in the warmest
colors of my own feet.

Man Playing a Bue Guitar
My father,
blue man playing a guitar,
Picasso's Blue Man on a wall, in paint
outlined by straight lines,
confined, framed—
inside, lines of vision freely roaming
around the colored strokes, aimlessly.
I can hear him plucking a song,
following the notes to wherever they lead him,
a bricoleur on a stringed box,
plucking, plucking, plucking,
following the Muse,
playing.

Comment: When I first read the original, I loved the intense voice of Brooks' *Hunchback Girl*, and I wondered how students would hear it, how they would listen, what they would pull out of this bittersweet portrait. I was not surprised by the strong first person voices that emerged from the Re-creations, but I was surprised at the directions they took, from self to other—from God, the Father (as in the original), to human fathers, to lovers, to the content of paintings.

What I Am Not plays directly off the original, affirming the need for uniqueness, ending in the line "my own two feet," affirming the human necessity to count, to suffice, to be grounded in the self. *Conversation with My Father* personalizes the experience of the original, grieving momentarily for the loss of a father never really known. *Choosing* turns the experience into a love relationship, pleading for directness, honesty. *Man Playing a Blue Guitar* builds on allusion, invoking Picasso's painting *Man Playing a Blue Guitar*, using the words of the original to flesh out the imagination: *straight, confined, framed*, to characterize his father who turns out to be a free spirit *following the Muse*, after all. Each illumination, written in less than three minutes, is magical.

> Facts [are] not separate things...but an everchanging pattern against a boundless background of the unknown, an immense kaleidoscope changing constantly according to the different ways you looked at it.
>
> —Joanna Field,
> *A Life of Ones Own*

What seems to be activated in the process of Re-creation is the mind's synthesizing ability in the absence of full information. Improvisation in three minutes or less activates the pattern-seeking part of the brain sensitive to image, metaphor, nuances of feeling to become connective, multi-directional, contextual. The resulting writing is nothing short of amazing, giving students a sense of empowerment which carries over into their writing life.

Complexity and Re-creations

Let's look at the qualitative responses to two highly complex poems, in addition to their length. I first experimented with a famous poem, *Thirteen Ways of Looking at a Blackbird* by Wallace Stevens, who is considered a *difficult* poet, in a graduate class. The poem consists of thirteen stanzas of two to three epigrammatic lines each.

The graduate English major of the following piece was so *startled* by the unconventional nature of the activity and by my request to write no more than three minutes—and without having the poem in front of her that, in her words, she unwittingly *unhooked* from everything she had learned during several years as an English major, going on *automatic*, and produced these lines, to her *total shock*.

Variation on a Theme

Black bird.
Black bird.
Waiting, waiting,
his eye rotating
moving over
20 snowy mountains,
his eye a reflection
of innuendos
as a river moving
frozen icicles forming
a glass coach, a
glass shadow of
rhythm that
carried a thin man
and sad woman
out of sight at
the edge of the
3 minds as they
moved into one:
the man and the
woman and, yes
the black bird
together in the
green light on
the cedar limbs.
Winds of fear
whirling, whirled,
erase the inflection,
the mood, the meaning.

Not until two years later did I dare to risk using the thirty-eight lines of *Thirteen Ways...* with freshmen, thinking the poem too difficult, too opaque, too convoluted. Although not as long as the graduate student's Re-creation, those of the freshmen—one and all—contained surprise after surprise:

Blind Minds
Barbaric shadows eat my imagination.
I have 3 blind minds, see how they fly.
Blackbird's world throws the bawds of
epiphany in the moving river.
A slight circle under the wandering eye
crosses man, woman,
and the mountains.
Blackbirds are written across New Jersey.
It was evening all afternoon
in Montana
in July, where blackbirds whistle
after man/woman and their
flooding eyes.
Here, cedar waxwings look
like dead leaves.
In Montana you can see their colors,
the ruby of their open mouths.
Here, there, blackbirds
are just black birds.

Blackbird Fear
Unvalued, misunderstood,
the blackbird circles and swirls
through our world.

The blackness, the mystery,
of the blackbird penetrates our fears,
transcends our realities.

We fear what we don't know.
We overlook what is common.
With busy, watchful eyes, the blackbird
exists whether or not we understand
or care.

The Way of Peace
The man, woman,
and blackbird
become one
They are intertwined
in inescapable
rhythms
The snowy, moving mountain
has cradled the man, woman,
and blackbird.
No fear will pierce their hearts.
They only know
tranquility
in the shadow of
the snowy
moving
mountain

Black and White
When all seems to be white and good,
when all tries to blend in,
blackbird stands alone, moving.
The motion of a blackbird
is like a pantomime.
It puts a man and a woman
together in wholeness.
Blackbird is the shadow of beauty:
why do you look for beauty in gold?
True beauty is within black.
When river flows, the blackbird
flies upstream against the flow.
No white bird can draw circles in the sky
like the blackbird.
It sits on the cedar limb,
watching the white world, pitying.

The Number 13
13 times blackbirds are mentioned.
13 stanzas are presented.
Different seasons interchange.
Men and women intertwine,
men, women,
and blackbirds intertwine
in the woven threads of Fate.
Here, there, landing nowhere,
blackbirds are just the shadows
of black
cats

Comment: If listeners had attempted to focus with narrow attention, they would have been frustrated at the outset, quitting before anything would be written. Wide attention cycles around the melody, allowing listeners to play with whatever attracts them. Stevens' thirteen stanzas contain much recurrence of images and words, a characteristic which found its way into most of the Re-creations. No one Re-creation ignored the blackbirds, and most saw that there was a connection between blackbird, man, and woman—and mountain. Beyond that, the Re-creations move in wildly different directions. No writer is constrained to interpret *correctly* or to make immediate sense

WHAT WE CAN LEARN FROM THIS CHAPTER

Each Re-creation carries with it a sense of wholeness, completeness, coming full circle despite having been written in less than three minutes. Some Re-creations take a phrase as a point of departure and go off into one direction. Some Re-creations play with the sounds of words. One re-creator wrote: "As I listened, the poem seemed a little *spacey*, but it exists in a beautiful, windswept place, which I recognize; then I get there, after all, in what I write."

C•H•A•P•T•E•R•F•O•U•R

Discovering a Center

SINCE FEELING IS FIRST

> Because feelings form the underlying structural matrix of thought, they are the key to remembering, to recognizing patterns, and to generating new ideas.
>
> —William Gray

Any creative act is set in motion by the search for pattern. When we discover such a pattern and express it in some way, we experience aesthetic satisfaction. The word aesthetic, comes from the Greek root *aisthesis*, which means both *feeling* and *sensation*, suggesting the simultaneous awareness of the feeling world within and the sensate world-without. Einstein described the aesthetic experience as a feeling of "elation, joy, amazement when the inner feeling and outer expression are congruent." Such attunement allows us to draw personal meanings from the external world. We experience emotional pleasure when something *hangs together* for us. When we structure something aesthetically, we create personal meaning, and, with it comes profound pleasure. Aesthetic perception is the recognition of a whole before its parts.

For example, in learning to sing or play a particular song, if we have heard its melody several times before we learn how to play it, the notes become much easier to learn than if we would begin with the notes. More often than not, the human brain prefers a sense of the melody before tackling the job of sequencing the notes. This way we don't have to start from scratch. The melody comes not only from what has gone before us but from what we can gather and incorporate into our own patterns of meaning.

As living organisms, we are attracted to patterns. We recognize only those patterns that make sense to us. The very idea of living is to connect somehow to something that matters to us, to each one of us as thinking, feeling beings.

The Feeling Focus in Wide Attention:

David Gelernter says we have far more experience stored in our memory than we will ever see with narrow focus. In Re-creations, the heard original is not logically understood, but felt, which requires wide attention. Wide attention roves and probes, with no clue as yet about what goal to reach, what problem to solve, what idea, image, or feeling to follow. It associates by analogy: as we listen to the poem, it reminds us of an analogous event and—bingo—an affect link is created; a feeling about the heard piece produces a memory or an image that triggers feeling. The mind surfs. Sparks. Bridges. Leaps. Associates.

Illumination: The Startle Reflex

Being startled is accompanied by a sudden flow of emotion at something bigger than we are used to. It is a multi-dimensionality that we try to stem in the course of our daily lives. Disconnected images suddenly coalesce. Being startled often shocks us into abandoning a conventional linearity to embrace multiple perspectives. These open us to the multilogue of human experience—views of multi-dimensions. This window into the dizzying multiplicity of experience leads to proliferating perspectives of the heard piece. When we are startled into an illumination, we have listened and have recognized a feeling that is our own—and it feels good.

This feeling process in Re-creation is shaped by several simple actions:

1. We are told we are going to be DO-ing something with what we hear—which means we are more likely to listen. The mode will be wide attention because we don't know what that

something is. This very fact alerts us emotionally because we don't know what to expect.

2. So we listen globally to the whole with wide attention. At this point we may exhibit any number of qualities: perplexity, anxiety, excitement, fear.

3. We listen, knowing only that we will gather as yet scattered parts around a blank center. We are clueless as to any specific goal we are supposed to reach.

4. Only after listening twice do we *name* the blank center before us with the most dominant impression we can garner from our listening. We are discovering our own center, not someone else's.

5. We re-create in a very limited time-span. We write easily because we have nothing invested: no perfection, no *sense*, no publishing, no grade, no failure, no…no. So we improvise in the spirit of exploration and discovery, opening us to connecting with the heard piece in unexpected ways. There's nothing to turn in; nothing to own, nothing to claim, nothing to think we can't do it—we just do it.

6. After reading what we've written, we re-discover yet another aspect of our Re-creation by re-naming the whole, which in turn becomes the title of our Re-creation.

Notice in the Re-creations of Al Young's *Chemistry* that students universally tended to USE the technical aspects of *chemistry* only to support their tie-in to the emotional component of the poem.

Chemistry
Al Young

What connects me to this moon
is legendary, and what connects
the moon to me is as
momentary as the night is
long before it burns away like
that fire in the eyes of lovers
when, spent, they turn
from one another and fall against
the dark sides of their pillows
to let their blood color cool.

You too know well the nature
of our chemistry: 65% oxygen,
18% carbon, 10% hydrogen,
3% nitrogen, a touch of calcium,
phosphorus and other elements.
But largely (by 70%) we're water:
2 parts hydrogen to 1 part oxygen,
and mostly we're still all wet—
9 parts fear chained to 1 part joy.
Is this why we're given to drowning
ourselves in pools of tears,
long on sorrow and shallow on laughter;
drowning ourselves in sugar and salt
as it were, as we are, as the treasured
substance of a former fish's life
can never be technically measured?

This chemistry we swim and skim
is what connects all light with me
olympically, for real life
since will forever be proving
this radiant suspension to be love
in but one of its bubbling mutations.
Chemistry
One's connection to this universe—
is it really chemistry?
One's connection to the moon—
is it really chemistry?
Such chemistry, as the fire
in the eyes of lovers
that soon fall into the dark side
of their pillows—
where did their chemistry go?
Our bodies 90% this, 20% that,
truly it's all wet and full of
this % of fear & that % of joy.
The real science, the real chemistry
is in the chemistry
of understanding ourselves,
understanding love.

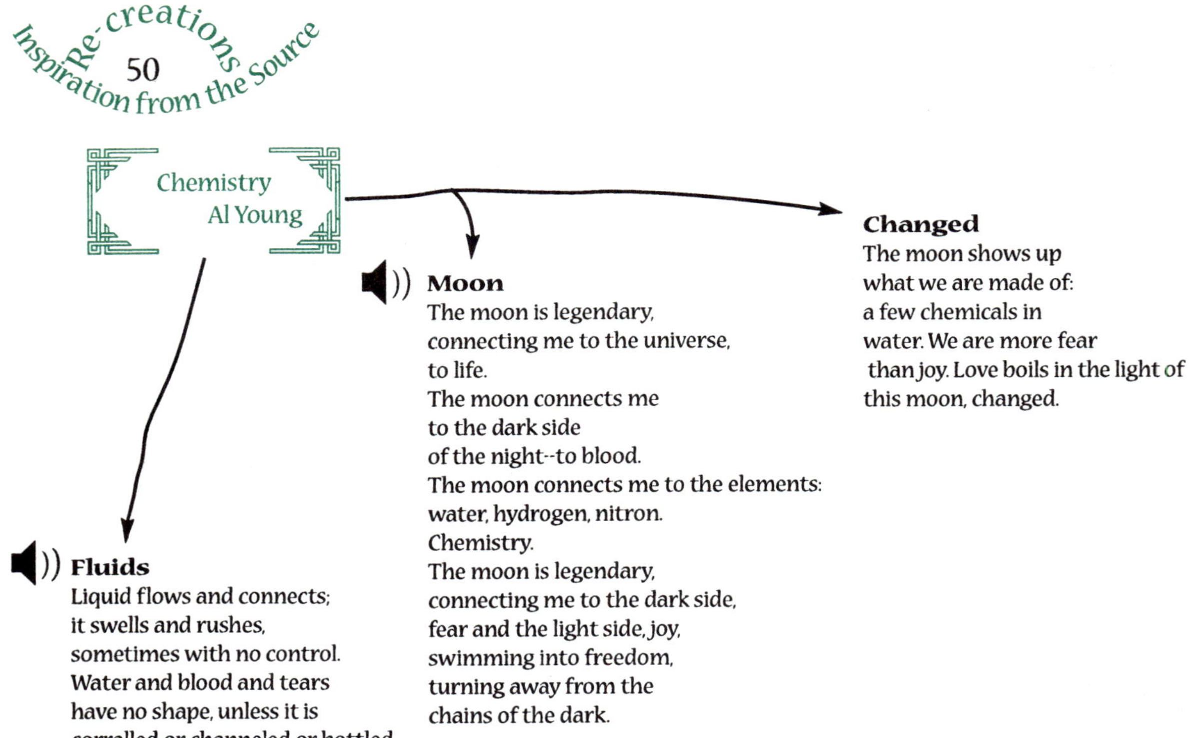

Inverse Clustering: Naming the Center, Re-Naming the Whole

Naming the center, the naming of a dominant feeling, then naming that which has been written in three minutes, continues the process of focusing on the whole. Shifting from the dominant feeling before the writing to naming the piece after it has been *written* reflects ownership: "These are *my* words. This is my pattern of meaning. This feels good." Although these writers are permitted to use the title of the original, few of them do. Surprised by what they were able to write, they do their *naming* of the title by drawing on their own content.

Feeling into Form

What is re-created is not the poem itself, but *what it FEELS like* writes philosopher Susanne Langer. In re-creating we perceive relationships, perceive a form, perceive significance which leads to evolving meaning as we associate examples of this feeling from our experience. It is whole-making, a total response, rather than an analytic response, that Langer insists, "cannot be paraphrased in discourse." A Re-creation is not a Re-creation of the poem but a Re-creation of the poem's emotive meaning to the listener in the moment of hearing.

Joanna Field, who, in exploring her own creative process in 1937, coined the phrase *wide and narrow attention*, describes the process this way: "Whatever I do there is always some central core of my thought standing out in a clear pattern against an all-enveloping vagueness… .But this core does not have clear-cut edges, it is not like the pattern of a carpet, stopping off short with a border. At any moment there exist in the fringes of my thought faint patternings which can be brought to distinctness when I look at them." Re-creations helps us approximate this tenuous process. Let's look at several originals and their Re-creations for hints of "the faint patternings" which have been brought to distinctness.

The Peace of Wild Things
Wendell Berry

When the despair of the world grows in me
and I wake in the night at the least sound
in fear of what my life and my children's life may be,
I go and lie down where the wood drake
rests in his beauty on the water, and the great heron feeds.
I come into the peace of wild things
who do not tax their lives with forethought
of grief. I come into the presence of still water.
And I feel above me the day-blind stars
waiting with their light. For a time
I rest in the grace of the world, and am free.

The Greatest Animal

Man thought he was the greatest animal because
men had New York. Men had airbirds & nuclear missiles.
The dolphins knew they were smarter because they didn't.
I have spent too much of my life
behind closed door
dwelling on possessions
dwelling on heady thoughts
while the trees contemplated the winter night
the heron laughed
and thought of a shell, perhaps
I worry about bills and taxing mind
with self-important matters of the word
till I go to Williams Street Park
and look at the trees
and the few stars San Jose
will let through
(realize all the important things)
are just living and being
without responsibilities.

Breaking through Walls

Fear: of life and failure
or new beginnings,
fear of tomorrows that may never come.
These things I take flight from,
leave this frenzied world
and enter the world of Nature.
Within her arms I feel
the cooling of a subtle breeze
or the calm, continuous lapping of water.
At once I am at peace,
free to be an unexpected guest
in a land beyond the walls
of my daily confinement.

Get Me Away

Away from the skyscrapers,
away from the graffiti,
away from the horns, and buzzers,
and sirens
to Mr. Berry's world I go
alone:
To connect with my primordial being,
to connect with me,
to connect
with peace.

A Far Piece to Grace

It's a far piece to grace
sloshing among the ducks
at night, bitten by unseen
bugs, whipped by dark reeds
guarding dull waters,
surface-lit by silver
but, below,
solid lead.
We are waiting for light,
unbreathing,
immobile,
waking entangled
in unshakeable consciousness.
I'd sleep in Frosted wood,
horse or no horse,
not caring whose they were,
and not wait for light.

Listening

Often my sheets
have wrapped around me
barring escape.
In such moments there exists
a window between that which is seen
and that which is heard.
Even as my four walls
enclose my body,
I will look through the window
and find the wild things—
all that which has escaped,
and in such an intellectual silence
I listen.

The Love of Now

Uncertainty and despair enslave us.
We live our desperate lives trying just to survive.
Yet we are freed in the stillness
and simplicity of the world's beauty.
We can escape from an ever-changing
uncertain tomorrow:
a simple joy of birds, sunsets, and stars.
The life of tomorrow may seem dark,
but simple pleasures today enlighten us
with peace.
There is freedom in simplicity and rest.
We can rest and look for tomorrow
with hope.

Comment: These Re-creations of Wendell Berry's poem become intensely personal, ranging from *listening* to the cry, *get me away* to *breaking down walls*, as if the poet had tapped into something primordial within these writers.

Those Winter Sundays

Robert Hayden

Sundays too my father got up early,
and put his clothes on in the blueblack cold,
then with cracked hands that ached
from labor in the weekday weather made
banked fires blaze. No one ever thanked him.
I'd wake and hear the cold splintering, breaking.
When the rooms were warm, he'd call,
and slowly I would rise and dress,
fearing the chronic angers of that house.

Speaking indifferently to him,
who had driven out the cold
and polished my good shoes as well.
What did I know, what did I know
of love's austere and lonely offices?

Divorce

Sundays were my day with him.
We read the funnies, both of us in our jammies,
but the cold, cracked hands of doubt and hate took him away.
I never had a Sunday again.
I felt alone in love's lonely office.
He left me to cry.
I never got to say good-bye.
He only said, "I don't love mommy anymore."
He spoke indifferently to me.
My heart fell out of my chest,
onto the cold floor, breaking and splintering.
Even today, Sundays are always a loss for me.

Revenge

Black as night does
your cold heart rise,
splintering the minutes of my life
breaking all my rules.
It does anger me so
to know you didn't want me.
With fire I'll polish your soul.

Legacy

Father,
is it too late to thank you,
to take the gnarled hands that always
held me so gently and kiss them
for showing me what the hands
of a kind man are like?
It is your lonely life that taught me
how to find love in another man's hands.

Afraid

On a cold Sunday morning.
I wake up with fear.
My body is still aching from last week's beating.
Father is home all day.
I'll have another black eye.
No one ever thanked me for
putting out his anger.

Your Austerity

Father,
I never thanked you
for warming my body
and polishing my shoes.
If only we could have talked,
but only indifferent speech
came to our lips
and cold, splintery thoughts
to our minds.
If only we could see beyond
the blue-black anger
and your cracked hands
to the love held down
by austerity and loneliness.

Resentment

Those winter Sundays,
the house cold,
my eyes heavily closed,
my sleep broken gently
by the nudging noises
of my father
waking the house:
the light's turned on,
the heat turned up,
the doors opened.
I pretended not to hear,
pretended sleep
and resented
the intrusion.

Church Anger

On Sundays, always, he rose
early before we did
cracked and weathered knuckles
securing the alien cuff-links.
How I hated Sundays, too,
rising in the blue-black cold as
if it were a school-day.
Church days we travelled far,
the car running on chronic angers
fueled by mother's silent depression
and father's righteousness
I only wanted peace,
but what did I know?

Strangers

My father was unable to show his love.
We walked like strangers in the house on a cold winter's Sunday.
I in my youth, my old father a creation of his hard labor.
Fire and ice, youth and age, together yet so far apart.
Loneliness speaks loudly.

Dad

Thanks, Dad
for driving me to games
working overtime to get me shoes
on those painfully cold mornings
in Michigan,
no one near to say thanks.
Damn, I should say it more.
I need to tell you now
how much I respect you,
how much I admire you
how much I need you
You've made so much of me,
I wonder, can I really succeed?
I never want to disappoint you.
This one's for you.
Can I do it?
I need help, time, love,
I need Dad.

Still Lonely

You, my father, wearing blue-black clothing,
making your form difficult to see in the early morning light,
warming the rooms of our house,
the cracking, splintering wood snapping in the fire.
Yet, and yet, you leave cold the rooms of our hearts
where chronic angers freeze the very marrow where blood is formed.
You want no thanks,
no outward show of love for the labor of your hands.
Are you lonely? I am. We are.

Carpenter

I awake in the blue-black of morning with aching hands and aching legs, scared as I always am before the dark lifts. Even the warm licks of my dog, her eyes welcoming me out of sleep, do not comfort my anxiety. I will be OK a couple of hours from now, when I reach my place of labor, wrapped safely in my tool belt. I will carry lumber and pound nails and miss my dogs and be thankful I do not work in lonely offices.

Comment: How can anyone doubt the feeling focus engendered by this original piece? Perhaps the emotional impact of the original makes it more difficult to escape the *father* figure of the original poem, whoever he was or wasn't, is or isn't, in each Re-creator's life. There is an emotional weight of loss, of regret, even of bitterness, as well as gratefulness in these Re-creations. The outer, the original poem, triggers the something of the inner emotional life of the listener, which is discovered when the blank center is named, and owned when the vignette is re-named.

Letting Go

Screaming with laughter, you move away from me. I sprint to keep up, but fall further behind. I close my eyes and wait for the thud that tells me you need me. It doesn't come, and as my mouth rounds in surprise, I open my eyes and realize you are waving goodbye. My heart becomes more breakable in that millisecond of realization. My fear and understanding lope after your distant figure until I call them back, smile, and wave my hand in return.

To My EX

I left, jaw set, eyes on the horizon,
You wept, eyes on yourself.

You knew not your power to become;
I renounced my right to grieve.

Time softens, lets sighs go, sets sights.
I weep for what we had.
You set your sights on your future.

Goodbye Ride

Loping through life,
I taught myself to look ahead,
look ahead before the thud of
reality wobbles the brain.
I told myself: Now I ride on,
smaller, more breakable, wobbling,
into the past.
I've been thudded enough.
Goodbye, future,
Goodbye, ride.
I'll lope through life.
You take the thud.
Wobble it once for me.

The Balance

I see the distance.
Flapping, I try to ride there.
To my surprise—thud.
But I am not breakable.
I continue to ride,
wobbling but riding.
I see the distance.
Round and round,
flapping and wobbling,
until—
I see the distance,
strength, power,
round and round,
pushing and pushing
until. . .
I am in the distance.

To A Daughter Leaving Home

Linda Pastan

When I taught you
at eight to ride
a bicycle, loping along
beside you
as you wobbled away
on two round wheels,
my own mouth rounding
in surprise when you pulled
ahead down the curved
path of the park,
I kept waiting
for the thud
of your crash as I
sprinted to catch up,
while you grew
smaller, more breakable
with distance,
pumping, pumping
for your life, screaming
with laughter,
the hair flapping
behind you like a
handkerchief waving
goodbye.

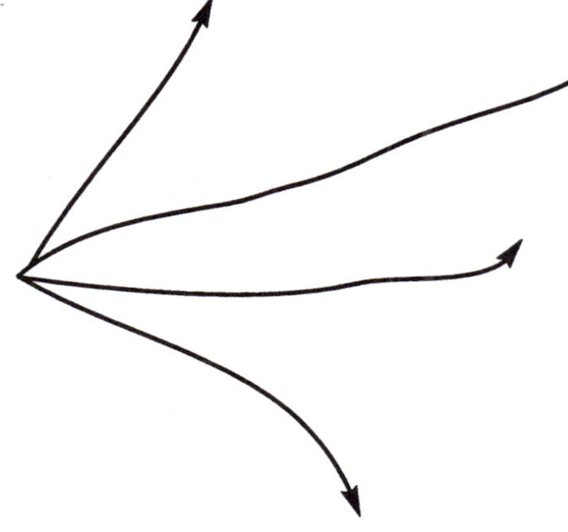

Goodbye
I saw it first in your eyes—
how they rolled sarcastically
  in their sockets,
and then in the way your hips
curved to indicate
you disagreed.
And then, in dreams,
you, spinning round and round,
trying to cast yourself out of
my orbit, trying to resist
my gravitational pull.

Breakable
Thin-paned glass
always seemed
sturdy enough
until my hanging hand—
knocking on the window—
shot out from beneath
my vampire robe.
I didn't have the chance
to feel it give,
my arm rushing past
the broken shard,
moistened clean rip
along my arm,
bleeding in the hallway,
me staring at the glass
grating underneath me.

Parting
Parting isn't easy,
yet it delights the soul.
You're sad for the times that passed,
happy for the experiences that await you.
You build your life
stone by stone
using your past as the base
that supports all.

Lessons
When I was eight, I heard the crash of a car.
That auto hit a ten-speed bike, similar to mine.
I remember pumping faster and faster and faster
to get to the accident.
Then I pushed my bike home.

When I was eight, I felt the throbbing thud
of a baseball bat, as I slid into home plate.
My base coach told me to stay at third,
but I knew I could make it.
"You're OUT" is all I remember of baseball.

When I was eight I hated my parents.
They made me eat and do things I didn't like.
I wish I could have that time back.
That was the final lesson.

Comment: Note the extreme variation in emotional timbre of these Re-creations of Linda Pastan's poem. Note also that each Re-creation is written in the first person. The design of each is whole, complete—a configuration, despite the fact than the writing activity lasted less than three minutes.

In the following original, note that, even a poem that is deliberately vague and sophisticated allows the listener to hone in on the essence of the following poem: the mystery, the uncertainty, the ambiguity of *love*.

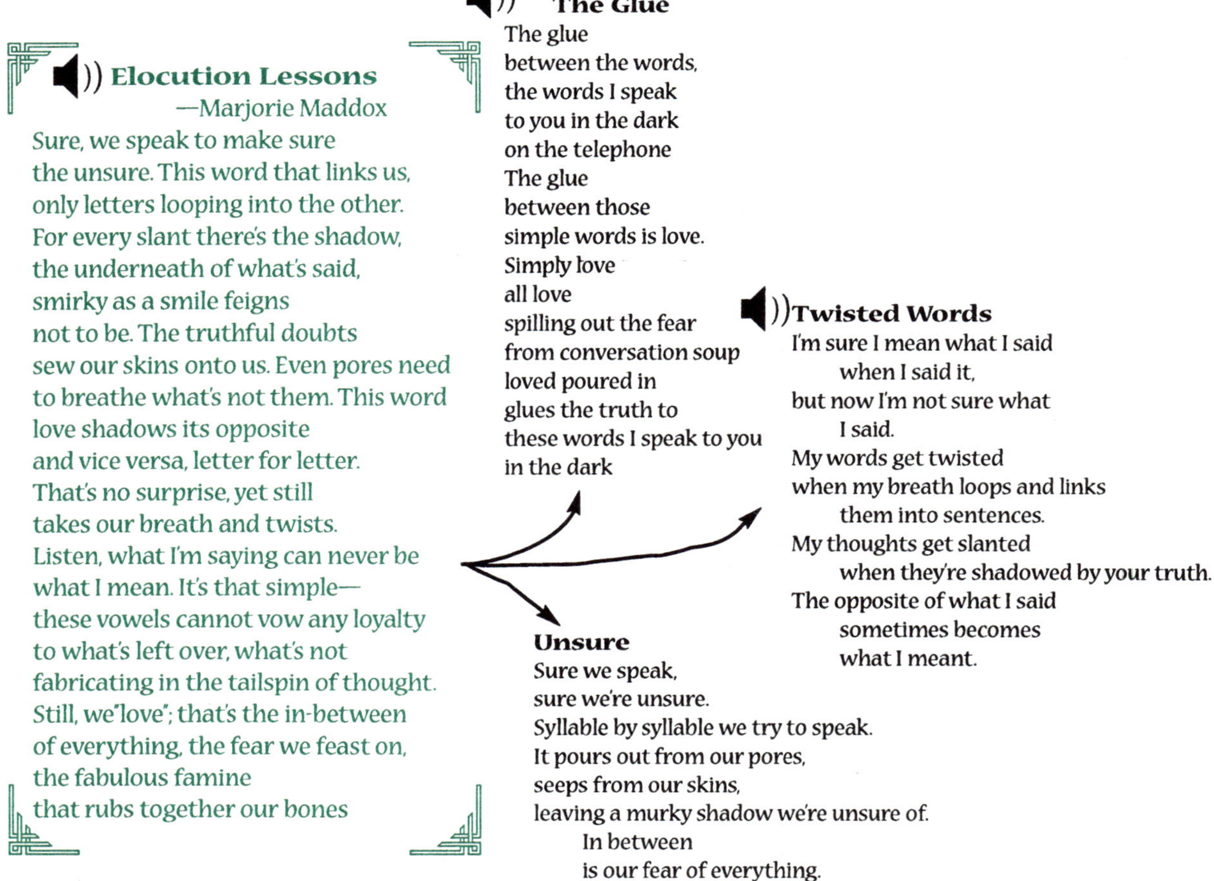

What We Can Learn from This Chapter:

The original piece, coming from the outside in as we listen to it being read, serves as the trigger to our own discovery of a center of personal meaning, whose movement is from the inside out. The two movements— from outer to inner, from inner to outer—meet in the naming of the center which was initially left blank.

We draw inspiration from a source because we are permitted to connect with its feeling-core on our own terms. We name what we feel or perceive as significant in what we heard. Naming this feeling to fill the blank center jump-starts the process of activating the creative potential inherent in each one of us, and each according to our abilities. Re-naming it as the title allows us to own what we have written. In so doing, we reconnect with our creative potential, knowing we are all capable of expressing something that moves us, no matter what our skill level (Henry Van Dyke noted the world would be a silent place if only those birds who sang best were allowed to sing.)

> An ulcer is an unkissed imagination taking its revenge for having been jilted. It is an undanced dance, an unpainted watercolor, an unwritten poem. It is a sign from the humanity of the human that a clear spring of joy has not been tapped and must break through, muddily, on its own.
> —John Ciardi

I have great empathy—and a deep pity—for human beings who have not learned—or remembered from childhood—how to be creatively expressive in some medium. It is a key to emotional health and to the pleasure we feel when we have been able to produce something on a page. When this expressive path is blocked, it must break through, muddily on its own, as hinted at by this eighth grader's arresting statement:

> I keep my feelings pretty bottled up inside me. Sometimes I will build up to a point where I can't stand it anymore. Then I vent my frustrations through football. I just love trying to hurt people. What will I do when I don't play football anymore? I don't know. (Name withheld)

Re-creations are nothing more than a way of connecting with our natural desire for creative expression and a way of breaking through the learned creative helplessness which pushes too many into destructive expression of this drive. Creative expression is an *entering into* process, not an *observing* process. We cannot be just spectators. Little or big, it serves us to help us remember what we CAN be, what we CAN do as human beings—each and every one of us, and that it honors in us that impulse which pushes us beyond our limited boundaries into a wider awareness of our potential. My colleague James Conner sent me a fifteenth Century Teo Lei poem entitled simply

RESPECT

Respect for the kind
of intelligence that enables
grass seed to grow grass,
the cherrystone
to make cherries.

C·H·A·P·T·E·R·F·I·V·E

The Expanded Moment

THE POWER OF STORY

> When I was little, I used to draw disparate objects on a piece of paper—toasters, baseballs, flowers, what-not—and connect them with lines. These little connections are the beginning of every story.
>
> —John Updike

To learn to speak is to learn to tell a story, and stories are experiences that human beings contextualize in language. Stories, according to psychobiologist Renée Fuller, are at the heart of human intelligence: the ability to connect ideas and events in some meaningful way. Stories provide a context to help people relate what they already know with what they've just heard. We understand the one by re-contextualizing in terms of the other.

> We talk about. . what may be, or what we'd like to do,... leaps and crosslinks and spiderwebs between here and there, between then and now,...a continual weaving and restructuring of the remembered and the perceived and the imagined.
>
> —Ursula LeGuin

Contrary to some unrealistic expectations, the mind is not a straight thinker. The mind expands (and contracts) unevenly as it pursues patterns of meaning, in short, a story line. Psychobiologist Renee Fuller hypothesized in 1972 that the *story* is the smallest unit of memory; therefore, the human memory is story-based. Because story functions as the brain's most fundamental cognitive organizer, Fuller believes it to be neuroscientist Karl Lashley's *lost engram*. As a researcher, she has studied and written about the centrality of *story* in human knowing for many years. Our possession of flexible brains sophisticated enough to story our experience in language rather than merely to respond to our genetic programming has allowed us to expand our creative intelligence to invent and use computers, to build skyscrapers and airplanes, to develop medicines, and to leave human footprints through the creation of the arts.

Artificial Intelligence guru Roger Shank insists that our interest in telling and hearing stories is clearly related to the nature of intelligence because knowledge is a combination of experience and stories; memory, according to Shank, is nothing more than memory for stories, and stories are nothing more than especially interesting prior experiences. Creating a story, written or oral, lays down memory structures that will contain the gist of the story for the rest of our lives.

The essence of story is the sound byte, according to Renée Fuller. The sound byte allows our minds to build a bigger story around it, using images, feelings. The sound byte is like a pebble dropped into a pond. The images ribble from it, and its elaboration turns into a larger story. The cognitive advantages of a sound byte, are that a)it can't leave our minds, b) it is communication at its most compressed (thus poetic) and, c) it is an engram of *story*—enabling us to retrieve the gist of it in memory, then reconstruct its pattern. Most interesting here is that no one ever retells a story verbatim. So it becomes a variation on a theme which we want to tell because it has an emotional link.

The Story as Emotional Engram

Because the impulse to story may be emotional in origin, story is much more than merely a cognitive unit: "It is the extension of our emotional selves with an extraordinary capacity to elicit every emotion known to our species" Fuller tells us that "...the association of emotion and cognition links the richness of our emotional life to the richness of our intellectual capacity." The linkage between emotions and the stories they elicit raises possibilities about how memory is stored and retrieved. Fuller believes stories are stored and retrieved according to emotional category. The greater the emotional mix the more ways they can be accessed.

Years ago, at the Stanford Medical School's pathology lab, I held in my two hands the brain of a man who had just died. I must have described this, to me, awesome experience to one of my creative arts classes, explaining how the newly dead brain in my hands was a delicate pink, not gray at all. In the Writer's Notebook of one of my students, I found this entry:

> Looking at the black-and white photographs of the human brain in your book, I think back to the time you told us you actually got to hold one in your hand—a recently dead one, not a pickled one. And, now, as I try to copy its shape from your book, I can't help but be drawn to its beauty. I see so many things in its compact, split—but united—sphere: the dark and light crevices, the shadows which highlight cloud masses, or rolling mountains, or rippling water, the contours that trace a woman's belly and breasts, or that trace out hundreds of humans involved in a dance, their naked backs facing outward, showing spiral lines that bend and curve in endless motion. All these lines and curves touch each other, come together, forming the total shape of the brain which looks like a large walnut or a giant abalone shell from the sea—both holding life inside.
>
> And why, as I draw it, color it, move my hand to follow its bends and curves, do I feel so soothed? —Christina Drop

> Human memory is story-based. Not all memories are stories. Rather, stories are especially interesting prior experiences, ones we learn from.
>
> —Roger Shank

Harvard cognitive psychologist Howard Gardner argues that, as we grow, we become the stories we tell of our lives. And Roger Shank reminds us that memory is essentially memories for stories. When we retrieve a memory, we do so by certain indexes of story patterns in our experience that allow us to re-cognize—to know again—stories that are similar.... We retrieve or create a story at the right time, correlating it with one we already have indexed. This is the associative leap that happens in Re-creations.

> The extreme expression of the Kalahari Bushman's spirit was in his stories. The story was his most sacred possession. These people know what we do not, that without a story you have not got a nation, or a culture, or a civilization. Without a story of your own to live, you haven't got a life of your own.
>
> —Laurens van der Post, anthropologist

The story as engram suggests that everything we might ever want to say has already been thought up. But stories vary. No stories are ever identical over time.

Inventing a story—any story, is a process of adaptation. "Invention," says Roger Shank, "is not a process that comes from nowhere." It is massaging of old stories into new ones. We do this to discover coherence.

In doing so, we begin to understand the stories of others by adding aspects of our own lives that allow us to read into them what is most meaningful for us, and what is most meaningful has an affect-link. In the process, the Re-creation becomes a story in its own right—our own.

Engaging in Re-creations is a way of laying down memory traces. It is a way of, powerful learning. We take in someone else's *story* as we listen, but we do more. Our brains focus on a gist which has some kind of emotional pull on us because we relate this gist to our own lives. This gist, internalized in our own context, our own ever-expanding world map, makes retrieval possible.

The gist we have focused on (it might be another for another listener) is never an exact match but an *approximation* of what fits our context. The more flexible our brains, the less we reject the gist as something that *doesn't make sense* to us. Greater flexibility means greater ability to adapt it, find coherence where it isn't obvious that it exists, or invent coherence where it actually cannot be found. Then, with lightning speed, we integrate this gist into our expanding knowledge map.

> We understand events in terms of events we have already understood.
> —Roger Shank

This is the power of stories: we listen to them, read them, reconsider them, manipulate them, use them to understand the world and to operate in the world, adapt them to new purposes, tell them in new ways, reinvent them. We live in a world of stories. Our ability to utilize these stories in novel ways is a hallmark of what we consider to be intelligence.

Re-creations are an immediate and concrete example of this process. In re-creating, each of us decides almost instantly what to retain and what to discard—and thereby focus on what interests us so we can transform it into our own pattern, a pattern unique to us.

Human memory is a cluster of experiences. Finding a relevant past experience that will help make sense of a new experience—such as a poem being read for Re-creation—is at the core of intelligent behavior.

> We assess the intelligence of others on the basis of the stories they tell and on the basis of their receptivity to our own stories—and we view intelligence as being intimately bound up with the notion of understanding.
> —Roger Shank

> Reminding is the mind's method of coordinating past events with current events to enable generalization and prediction. . . .One can't be said to know something if one can't find it in memory when it is needed.
> —Roger Shank

When we hear a poem read, our mind organizes around what it recognizes, reaching here and there. We select out those qualities which fit, ignoring the rest, just as the children in Chapter 1 who painted their favorite painting focused on what had an emotional pull for them and ignored what was too complex for them or what they did not yet have the skill for.

Variations on the Mythic:

> The capacity to personify, mythologize, imagine, harmonize, improvise, is one of the great mercies granted in human life.
> —Stephen Nachmanovitch

The word myth comes from the Greek word mythos, meaning *tale*. These tales are both resonant and opaque, reflecting deep-seated human needs and feelings, so much so that the *tales* cross all cultural boundaries, seemingly wired into the collective memory of the human species.

> The Mythic journey is as ancient as the human race itself.
> —John A. Allen

Although many of us no longer recognize the allusions to myths, calling up the whole story rich in overtones and associations may activate a whole network of memories in us. Myth works like layers of an onion. Some of us peel back only the first layer; others of us can peel back many layers straight to a central core of understanding.

> What the mythtellers and the oral poets know is that truth cannot be captured in a solitary idea. It is alive and uncatchable. It tumbles about in the polyphonic stories told by the animals and birds and mountains and rivers and trees...
> —Sean Kane

Here are Re-creations of a poem about Ulysses' wife Penelope. The story embedded in Millay's poem, re-created by learners, made them much more receptive to learning something about *The Odyssey.*

Penelope
An ancient gesture
made by Greeks, and others, past and present,
overcome by tragedy, real or imagined.
Tears are that gesture of sadness,
sagging frame bent over in grief,
the body wracked with convulsions, endless tears
washing away waves of emotion,
a release, a catharsis, very Greek.

Penelope
That morning I woke
wrapped in sheets feeling
regal—your Penelope.
The words you spoke
shocked me senseless.
You, my Ulysses, were not
too moved
by my tears to speak.
You with your ancient gesture—
spit at my face 'til my hair
was wet
with hate hung limp.
My husband, really gone.
The twisted sheets strangled
me—
death would be a relief.
I never really cried, did you?

Penelope
Who are the ones that really cry,
the others whom fame eludes?
Whose gestures go unnoticed,
ancient, without recognition?
Penelope woke to the light each morning
tired, worn, and alone,
weaving in vain to fill what they shared
while he sailed further and further away.

Penelope
Tonight I hang my apron
on the peg of the antique cupboard
for the last time.
The apron has grown tight,the nights
have grown long,
the weaving is finished.
The Greek bands of blue
are the color of the Mediterranean
The white linen threads
tell the story of
loss.

An Ancient Gesture
Edna St. Vincent Millay

I thought, as I wiped my eyes on the corner of my apron:
Penelope did this too.
And more than once: you can't keep weaving all day
And undoing it all through the night;
Your arms get tired, and the back of your neck gets tight;
And along towards morning, when you think it will never be light,
And your husband has been gone, and you don't know where, for years,
Suddenly you burst into tears;
There is simply nothing else to do.

And I thought, as I wiped my eyes on the corner of my apron:
This is an ancient gesture, authentic, antique,
In the very best tradition, classic, Greek;
Ulysses did this too.
But only as a gesture,—a gesture which implied
To the assembled throng that he was much too moved to speak.
He learned it from Penelope...
Penelope, who really cried

Penelope
Where the road seems to peter out
again, trail aimlessly,
the work undone by will,
undone by desire,
I go back, retrace my steps
to the source.
I am most of all
alone, futile,
human.

Here is a poem which makes an allusion to the story of Icarus, the boy who flew too close to the sun, a tale from Ovid.

To a Friend Whose Work Has Come to Triumph
Anne Sexton

Consider Icarus, pasting those sticky wings on,
testing that strange little tug at his shoulder blade,
and think of that first flawless moment over the lawn
of the labyrinth. Think of the difference it made!
There below are the trees, as awkward as camels;
and here are the shocked starlings pumping past
and think of innocent Icarus who is doing quite well;
larger than a sail, over the fog and blast
of the plushy ocean he goes. Admire his wings!
Feel the fire at his neck and see how casually
he glances up and is caught, wondrously tunneling
into that hot eye. Who cares that he fell back into the sea?
See him acclaiming the sun and come plunging down
while his sensible daddy goes straight into town.

Playing It Safe
I'll play
I'll play
I'll put on the wings
I'll spread them across the canyon
I'll cast a shadow on the desert
I'll fly next to an eagle
I'll melt into a cloud
I'll touch the sun
I'll play
I'll play
it safe
from under a tree
on the edge of a mountain.

Judgment
See the hot eye staring,
its burning gaze seeing through you.
Think of how it makes its judgment.
See the hot eye, bright with
opinion,
wide-open and crippling.
Think of how it knows you.

No Daddy, She
My friend plunges
into words
off the fog-shrouded coast
into the hot eye
of her own voice—
this starling of a poet,
this startling friend/lover,
her words begin where mine
leave off.

Extremes
I live at the extremes,
in cold places of one thing or the other.
I'm blind to the middle.
Again I will fly
up toward that necessary flow,
and again the wax melts.
Again and again.

Not Knowing

My linear, logical left brain needs its daily dose of definition. Why can't I remember the legend of Icarus? It is as blocked as my creativity. He seems to be the key to unlocking the meaning of that poem. Without him, I am on the outside looking in..

Foreign Language Student
To start writing makes a difference,
but awkward.
Idea is larger than a sail,
wide enough to be ocean.
To confess makes me fear,
like being in fire.
My ideas are branches of a tree
but sticky wind takes them away.

Comment: *Foreigh Language Student* is by a young woman who came from Japan to study in America. She was fearful of speaking, of writing, especially terrified of the swiftness of Re-creations. For the first time in her life, she was released from the fear as she experienced the freedom of improvisation—and it opened her to tell her own story.

Here is a *story* of World War I by a poet who served in it and died a young man:

Dulce et Decorum Est

Wilfred Owen

Bent double, like old beggars under sacks,
Knock-kneed, coughing like hags, we cursed through sludge,
Till on the haunting flares we turned our backs
And toward our distant rest began to trudge.
Men marched asleep. Many had lost their boots
But limped on, blood-shod. All went lame; all blind;
Drunk with fatigue; deaf even to the hoots
Of tired, outstripped Five-Nines that dropped behind.

Gas! Gas! Quick, boys!—An ecstasy of fumbling,
Fitting the clumsy helmets just in time;
But someone still was yelling out and stumbling,
And floundering like a man in fire or lime...
Dim through the misty panes and thick green light,
As under a green sea, I saw him drowning.
In all my dreams, before my helpless sight,
He plunges at me, guttering, choking, drowning.

If in some smothering dreams you too could pace
Behind the wagon that we flung him in,
And watch the white eyes writhing in his face,
His hanging face, like a devil's sick of sin!
If you could hear, at every jolt, the blood
Come gargling from his froth-corrupted lungs,
Obscene as cancer, bitter as the cud
Of vile, incurable sores on innocent tongues—
My friend, you would not tell with such high zest
To children ardent for some desperate glory,
The old Lie: Dulce et decorum est
Pro patria mori.

Dying for War is Beautiful?

Yea, sure, tell that to the dead guy who used to live a peaceful life until he got drafted and was forced into "the Man's" war. The quote should mean: what a crappy thing it is to die for one's country in a war another man started. What a crappy thing it is to die in a war forced upon you.

Honor and Pride

A purple heart is what my husband got for his bravery. A measly badge and a piece of paper in return for the loss of all four limbs and his ability to speak. I sit and look at him while he sleeps. I wonder if the honor they bestowed on him makes the hurt go away? I wonder if he is still proud of serving his country. The answer is all too sick to comprehend. For when he is in the study, the place where I've hung his war and military memorabilia at his request, his eyes are on fire. His aura bursts with pride. I weep.

> From listening to the stories of others, we learn to tell our own.
>
> —M. Atwood

Below are Re-creations of a *story* of the disintegration of a marriage by Adrienne Rich, a Re-creation of which, *Photography*, we encountered in Chapter 1.

Dissolve in Slow Motion

Alicia Suskin Ostriker

When you watch a marriage
Dissolve, in slow motion,
like a film, there is a point
Early on when the astute
Observer understands nothing
Can prevent the undesired
End, not shrinks, or friends,
Or how-to-love books,
Or the decency or the will
Of the two protagonists
Who struggle gamely like lab
Mice dropped in a jar
Of something viscous: the
Observer would rather snap
The marriage like a twig,
Speed the suffering up, but
The rules of the lab forbid.

Other rules govern decay
From within; so she just watches:
The little paws claw
Then cease, the furred
Bubbles of lungs stop.
The creatures get rigid.
Has something been measured?

A Story
Marriage:
the beginning for some,
the ending for others.
Observers look on
wanting and wishing
things will end.
But the tie that was created
cannot be cut by others.

Snap
Ridged creatures.
Two protagonists
snap like a twig
moving in slow motion.
Marriage dissolves.
Undesired end.

Marriages
Mice are misunderstood.
Rats don't scrabble
in slo-mo; they chew
through rules, their claws
pause on the lips of jars
filled with odd liquids,
sniff & reject
the effluvia of decay.
Rats defer mice.
Mice prefer rats.
Marriage provides a larger cage,
litter, and the remnants
of eaten mice.
Later, more mice,
& the same rats.

Angst
Thrown away—
its what happens to us all.
But we still suffer
through the anguish of the unknown
and the known.
Onlookers weep or laugh,
seeing their own turmoil played out before them
knowing they are the next
to be
discarded.
We look on with Angst.

Yes or No?
Mom's shrink says to...
Dad's friend says to...
The love books say to...
It slips away, even with outside help.
They feel like lab mice.
Does it really matter?

Watching and Waiting
Rigor mortis has set in.
Once there was life in this shell of a marriage.
Now its breathing has stopped
You watched with patient impatience,
You watch and whisper,
waiting for that tense moment
of indecision, knowing
you can influence the final scene.
As the unraveling begins,
you snap your fingers.

Botched
Sometimes a marriage
dissolves slowly like
a film.
The observers can
understand nothing
from outside,
watching the two
protagonists suspended
in slow air, sinking
and churning, gasping
until they surrender.
They are a botched experiment,
measuring nothing.
You try, I try.

Always Off
But we are always trying
at different times.
Those who watch the dance
know the dancers will never be
in tune with the music
at the same time.
They are always off.
Each, trying in alternation,
prolongs the eventual death.

What We Have Learned:

Here's a *story* in sixteen little lines of such mythic dimensions that it speaks for more human relationships than we care to count:

The Story: How Fire Took Water to Wife

Lisel Mueller

You are telling a story:
How Fire took Water to Wife.
It's always like this, you say,
opposites attract.

They want to enter each other, be one.
So he burns her as hard as he can
and she tries to drown him.

It's called love at first
and doesn't hurt
but after a while she weeps
and says he is killing her,
he shouts that he cannot breathe
under water—

Make up your own
ending, you say to the children,
and they will, they will . . .

The story line here is concrete, sequential. Two people fall in love, marry, and fight. The story is also metaphorical: *Fire* and *Water* marry—they do not mix. It is also symbolic: *Fire* is male; *Water* is female. At the deepest level it is a story about the story of human beings which applies to all of us—and we make up our own endings, always. As we can see, a created artifact is not fixed, static, with one or two—even three or more—levels of meaning, but rather fluid, expandable and contractable as we, the listeners, resonate with it. We have to remember how powerful storying is to human cognition: All cultures story; just as all cultures make music and all cultures dance. The story is a potent reminder of the way in which the inner and outer, the individual and community, humans and their interaction with nature, are inextricably linked by a dynamic, rhythmic play of life forces.

All stories are stories of the multifacetedness of life. We can play with multiple versions of a stranger's story, a friend's story, our own stories, and we can play with our own story from a mythic, a chronological, an emotional, a metaphoric, an analytic similitude, among many possible similitudes. I'm not talking about a true version vs. a false version, but about the different variations of *story* which, depending on how we tell it, will always allow us creative choices in how we look at our lives—or someone else's life—or life in general. Moreover, this vision can —and will —change over time. How we saw our fathers at six is not how we saw them at sixteen, nor at twenty-six. Memory, like history is in an on-going state of revision.

> A re-creation allows the voice that already exists to resonate in the listener's mind.
> —Student

> Re-creating presents us with an already-created image for transmutation.
> —Student

> I never thought storytelling could be so easy.
> —Student

CHAPTER SIX

The Mind's Diversity

THE MANY WAYS OF MAKING MEANING

As if the human ability to make meaning weren't complicated enough to examine, there are many ways to make meaning out of what Alfred North Whitehead called *the blooming, buzzing confusion* characteristic of living systems. For example, the human mind recognizes patterns in the sounds of language, patterns in feelings, patterns in images, patterns in ideas. Among many others, sound, feeling, image, idea, are all possible patterns of connection.

Congruence; Melody; Elation:

Our in-built search for patterns of meaning is a way of knowing. The way we know is to discover coherence or congruence among aspects of our senses and our feelings, which combine when we are in a state of attention. When the attention is *wide*, (see ch. 3), we have a greater opportunity to grasp the melody, or overall pattern, preceding absolute recognition of what it is about. Wide attention disengages us from preoccupation with particulars, When we *get* a melody, we have perceived a pattern, whether are listening or are writing or have written. Sensing a melody brings with it a sense of surprised pleasure

The *melody* is perceived in a multitude of ways, but it is dependent on our sense of a pattern, a harmonious whole. We are suddenly aware that certain notes *go together*, bringing us pleasure. The melody can be primarily a pattern of sounds, a pattern of images, a pattern of ideas, a pattern of sequences (the basis of which is plot or chronology); patterns of physical movement (kinesthetic), pattern of feeling, or any combination of these. Scanning for patterns of meaning is the mind's way of discovering something congruent with what it already understands.

When we have listened to the already-created poem—the coherence of someone else's need to understand, we have already gathered a sense of melody in what we have just heard. This melody becomes a starting point for a thought stream in which our own parade of congruences occupies our minds. From there, what our minds choose to focus on as most significant has a layering effect: sometimes it is pure feeling; sometimes it is a dominant image; sometimes, a metaphoric leap to an idea; sometimes it becomes nothing more or less than a pattern of sounds. Nevertheless, all reaching toward coherence or congruence is the reaching for pattern, whatever the shape that pattern takes.

Varieties of Similitude: our in-built pattern detector.

> When there is no literal meaning, it is counterproductive to look for it; "affect linking must happen."
> — David Gelernter

SIMILITUDE is not identity; similitude is not sameness; similitude is not identity. Similitude is similarity without being identical, and it takes many variations. It is the mind's core ability to connect with another mind on something heard or with the natural world on something seen in a moment of understanding, and to be able to express this momentary understanding on some level: either in similar images, similar ideas, similar feelings, similar sounds—all of which synthesize—tacitly— an aspect of a learner's recognition of congruence.

Sound Similitude

If words speak to the mind or to the heart, they also speak to the ear. Words combine in patterns that make us want to listen. Children fall in love with words because of their sound. They learn to relish words, revel in the way they resonate, play with their sounds. When sound and sense intertwine, recognition happens. A recent example is a three year-old boy, in a furniture store with his parents who are waited on by a saleswoman named La Sonia. She asks his name and tells him hers. Sometime later, she asks him, "What's my name?" His search for congruence begins: "Ummmm…it's like, umm... (trying hard, a little shy, still searching) Your name is PASTA!" Recognition. Triumph. Pleasure. He had retrieved the pasta he knew, which was Lasagna! Here is a perfect example of sound similitude: La Sonia = Lasagna= Pasta. Wide attention. The already known wedded to the unknown. Transformation. Similitude. Creative response. Improvisation. Learning. Growth.

Glory be to God for dappled things—
For skies of couple-colour as a brindled cow;
For rose-moles all in stipple upon trout that swim;
Fresh-firecoal chestnut-falls; finches' wings;
Landscape plotted and pieced—fold, fallow, and plough;
And all trades, their gear and tackle and trim,
All things counter, original, spare, strange;
Whatever is fickle, freckled (who knows how?)
With swift, slow; sweet, sour; adazzle, dim;
He fathers-forth whose beauty is past change:
Praise him.

Praise Him

Praise Him who created all unique
freckled femmes with swift skirts
and an eye, blue, watching
each scar heal,
aroma of trout, or dung,
not only roses,
and the mole on her chin
again and again
make me smile.
Glory be to God.

The Lord's Work

The Lord's work is magnificent:
dappled colors of morning's rays
the fish's wishes to flow
and blow downstream;
tackle the tabernacle of life,
the counter, strange
range of the earth's low plains.
The swift winds blow
on the sea: I sit and wonder
what a magnificent creature
like me
he created.

Shall Not Be

And none shall be found here
amidst the incidental glory
of dappled needles and blossoms
among the fiery fresh coals
piercing the plowing green.
Mossy shadows,
the smudges of blue from streams
of silver spawns and ochre grays
shall not be sunk and snuffed
by man's god

Caught

Dappled sunlight forms trim lines on
the wings of a chestnut bird
stretching wings upward
in a strange ritual,
lifting beak in a majestic moment
caught for an instant in a change-speckled landscape,
lifting a voice
against the torrent of
silence
surrounding him.

Comment: The students who re-created Hopkins poem after hearing it read twice may not have been able to analyze the complexities of sprung rhythm, slant rhyme, or spondees, but they tacitly tuned into the sound pattern without prompting. Most of them re-created the melody of Hopkins' rhythms without any formal knowledge of how he wrote poetry, without ever having heard a single one of his poems until that moment.

Here are some playful approaches at sound similitude, using famous lines known for their powerful *sound-sense.* Play with them by taking one minute to re-create them on paper into your own expressions

Original:
The coming musk rose, full of dewy wine
The murmurous haunt of flies on summer eves.
—John Keats

Sound Re-Creation:
Summer evenings, dusky, dewy musk roses of failing light,
full, flushed with summer's faceted eyes, murmurous with sleep,
the flies, slow moving, stuporous in their haunt.

Original:
The moon, dwindled and thinned to the fringe of a fingernails
held to a candle,
Or paring of paradisiacal fruit, lovely in waning but lustreless,
Stepped.....
—Gerard Manley Hopkins

A cusp still clasped him, a fluke yet fanged him, entangled him,
not quite utterly.
—Gerard Manley Hopkins

Read these passages aloud and re-create, for one minute, the sounds of one of Hopkins' lines, taking only what wants to be taken, improvising as you can.

Emotional similitude:

Affect link, according to David Gelernter, is the "progenitor of all sane out of control mental experiences." With his broad experience in artificial intelligence hooked to his awareness of the tacit, the intuitive, and the improvisational, he argues that there is no low-focus (wide attention) thought without emotional charge. He is careful to explain that when we are in wide focus, we FEEL our thoughts. Wide focus hurtles us to other arenas of emotional color, highlighting an emotionally thematic, as opposed to an intellectually rigorous, pattern of logical arguments. Receiving an underlying emotional fragrance of one thing connected to another in one's experience leads inevitably to an emotional high which not only highlights congruence but involves the sequencing hemisphere as well in the act of DO-ing.

In Re-creations, the act of listening with wide attention, followed by clustering around a not-yet-identified center creates an affect link, leading to variations on an emotional theme. I can't think of another trigger that better illustrates affect link than Sharon Olds' *For My Daughter.* As I was experimenting with the amazing Re-creations students were producing, I wondered, "What in a poem strikes so close to the bone, is so unsettling, that their minds will shut down?" I was aware that I might sabotage my own process and the constant successes my students were having, but I had to find out. So I read a poem which confronts the emergence of sexuality. I read it again. I worried as they began to write. I was amazed at the congruences the students, primarily

sophomores in college of varying ages but mostly in the twenty-year-old range, discovered in less than three minutes of writing. I marveled at how much they understood, at how richly the human mind associates, appropriates, discards, and generates, its own patterns of meaning.

For My Daughter
Sharon Olds

That night will come. Somewhere someone will be
entering you, his body riding
under your white body, dividing
your blood from your skin, your dark, liquid
eyes open or closed, the slipping
silken hair of your head fine
as water poured at night, the delicate threads
between your legs curled like stitches broken. The
center of your body
will tear open, as a woman will rip the
seam of her skirt so she can run. It will happen,
and when it happens I will be right here
in bed with your father, as when you learned to
read
you would go off and read in your room
as I read in mine, versions of the story
that changes in the telling, the story of the river

Writing A Life
Daughter,
the beginning was
that gentle line slipped to your mother
like a page between a book's covers.
Here my love, you finish the story.
And now, who shall expose you
to the genetic authorship?
Who shall be your entry,
and what wonders shall you write?

Love and Lust
Jeffrey's it right now
(J. J. for short).
In first grade it's all innocence.
"I'm in love, Mom."
But one day there will be
someone,
hopefully someone special,
who will open your eyes
and your legs soon thereafter.
And then you will know
what a woman knows—
the sheer splendor of
two bodies moving as one,
most likely before you are ready.
My fingers are crossed
that there is also love.

Evolution
For My Daughter
I watch you sleeping softly in the night,
your liquid eyes not yet having seen,
covered only by the delicate membrane of your eyelids.
Within your body,
within your center,
lies a woman,
somewhere,
running as she will, along the bank
of a river which shifts its course,
always changing.
You ride its current,
and I watch
your blood's pulse at your temple,
you are so small,
so quiet,
so fragile.
Laughter flows from your heart
with love you do not yet
understand.
I wish you the best of journeys.

How It Is
He'll be
like a seam ripper
tearing through threads
formed over eons
for the express purpose
of being broken.

The Oldest Story
I've read the
versions:
It's always night
There are images of water:
liquid (eyes)
slipping (bodies)
water poured (together)
and metaphors of bodies (like father & mother)
body torn in the center so she can run
(and run and run)
the story of the river.

The Way It Is
There will be a day, mother,
when I will no longer
go to your room and
read in your bed.
There will be someone
who will look into my eyes
in the dark night
touching my silken hair
and my soft skin.
It will not be wrong.
He will take me tenderly,
not tear me like a seam of stitches,
hanging threads left behind,
showing damage irreparable.
Don't be afraid.

Comment: Wow! My fear that minds might shut down in the face of unwelcome, feeling-laden input was unfounded. The tacit knowledge we hold in memory leads to understanding far beyond anything most of us could explain logically. They all honed in on a tacit, archetypal experience and gave it expression, each in his/her own way, each with his/her own focus, her own center, her own emotional link (all writers in these examples were females). There were no unemotional Re-creations.

> Re-creations spark my emotions into rebirth. Merely knowing I will do something of my own with the poem I am hearing, I cannot hear it read without a cranking up of my feelings.
>
> —Student

Idea Similitude:

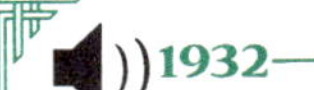

1932—

Linda Pastan

I saw my name in print the other day
with 1932 and then a blank
and knew that even now some grassy bank
just waited for my grave. And somewhere a gray

slab of marble existed already
on which the final number would be carved—
as if the stone itself were somehow starved
for definition. When I went steady

in high school years ago, my boyfriend's name
was what I tried out, hearing how it fit
with mine; then names of film stars in some hit.
My husband was anonymous as rain.

There is a number out there, odd or even
that will become familiar to my sons
and daughter. (They are the living ones
I think of now: Peter, Rachel, Stephen.)

I picture it, four integers in a row
5 or 7, 6 or 2 or 9:
a period; silence; an end-stopped line;

We Wait

You know my name,
you know my number
I have spent all of my life awaiting
that final digit death-day
to seal me up, close me in the annals.
My loves I tried on for "fit."
My husband, he was moonshine.
What I wanted most was fantasy.
I await my final digits
like a sledgehammer's "KABOOM."

Numbers

I know the date of my birth
as I know other numbers:
first phone number,
address to keep me from getting lost,
social security number,
driver's license,
my wife's office extension,
my mother's number I have to look up—
she moved once & look what happened.
I know my grandmother's grave
from the nearby tree,
the smell of the opened earth,
from the small nephew who cried in
bewildered uncertainty,
from the small cement cap with her name
& dates of birth & death
looking up into the sky
always now a little emptier,
an airy blue slab
revealing the anonymity
of odd numbers
carved in rain
& clothes in marching grass.

What We Know

As we grow, so does the grass in the field
where we will be returning.
No one knows its exact place or
the time of their arrival.
It is just a hope
that the grass will be long and lush,
and the marble slab will reflect the faces
of those we love.

Marks on Stone

Unknown is our final number.
The final year has your name.
The symbols of your birth and death are
defined on a slab of marble,
the only thing marking your existence.
Which name shall I take?
Odd or even, the odds are against you.

Definition—
Who am I?
What am I?
Dozens of madly differing
scenarios run
through my imagination.
The only sure one is my tombstone
solidifying
who I really was.

Forever Present
Over the threshold of blackness,
meeting with long-lost friends,
new kid on the block I am.
There's Homer, Sophocles,
Tina, and just ahead of me,
Uncle Johnnie.
The year is insignificant now.
Past, present, future are
foreign terms—
present forever I am.
It's the ultimate exploration;
no heavy equipment necessary.

A hammer delivers its final blow,
the final blow to the marked stone
rutting an end to my living.

Comment: We may never have had our birthdate printed in a book, as Linda Pastan has, but, as we listen to Linda Pastan's poem, we are drawn into recognition of the larger idea that we will also die. When we name the blank circle, our idea takes shape, and, when we write for three minutes, it takes a form on the page: we speak of the grass of our gravestone as *long and lush*, of the power of numbers *carved in rain*, of a husband who *was moonshine*. The potential for creative expression is activated every time.

> An idea is a feat of association.
> —Robert Frost

More often than not, Re-creations lead to speeded-up ideating. What we hear, what we listen to, is filtered through where we are in this moment, in this place, and nothing of what we hear sticks except that which has an emotional attractor to the as-yet unnamed center. The words and phrases we gather, like butterflies in a net, re-group our thoughts and images and feelings and stories into a new configuration of an abstract idea. Once we name it, we can re-create it in three minutes or less, radiating from the emotional center we have named. Once we write it, we can rename it to reflect what we have discovered in the writing. It becomes our idea, our awareness of something has changed in us that also has a resonance far beyond just our immediate selves.

> Abstract ideas are the patterns two or more memories have in common. They are born whenever someone realizes that similarity.
> —Rudolf Flesch

Image Similitude

Sometimes the congruence happens when image leaps to cohere with image. I remembered in my dissertation reporting on the responses of split-brain patients who were flashed an image to their right visual field (left hemisphere), then to the left visual field (right hemisphere), then given a series of objects to choose from to make a connection with what they had seen. Both hemispheres made clear connections; however, the kind of connection proved radically different. The left hemisphere, shown a whole chocolate cake on a plate, given a choice of many different objects to relate to the image they had just seen, chose such objects as a knife (to cut the cake with) or a fork (to eat the cake with). The same cake on a plate, flashed to the right hemisphere, made the split-brain patient select a round straw hat with a brim. The design mind chose a kind of shape-logic, an image-logic that had nothing to do with the sign mind cause-and-effect choices of the left hemisphere: we have a cake, we choose a knife in order to cut it or a fork so we can eat it.

Students re-created David Wagoner's *The Other House* and with their tacit knowing, zeroed unerringly in on the images that governed the poem, these images evoking a second layer of emotional similitude, with a third layer of sound similitude increasing the richness of the Re-creations.

The Richness of Being

Buildings have walls;
we form them to unrecognizable ______,
shape the molecules to our imagination.
But in an abandoned house
our efforts are grown over with green,
taken over with moss-smelling waters.
The wooden ribs become alive,
home for wet frogs, their dark home.
Light, we like to see
but to see, to feel in darkness is a better trick
I love Roethke's breathing cyclamens and smut.
I hate clean wood and stucco.

Haunted House

Not the other house
but this house
my house
haunts me. Four walls
ribbed, plastered, and painted
red on the inside, white
without. The roof's shingles
lay down like tufts of hair
needing a comb. In the deep
heart of my house
the old frogs croak
and squelch and I open
my mouth to hear them
in my throat—their chorus
sings of silence sought
but lost to the chaos
of a faucet's drip,
drip, dripping.
Sing frogs sing,
warm me within
against the worn weather
rubbing up against
my windows. Do not stop
that incessant churl
of throat, frogs,
for this house,
my house,
is the only house I know.

The Other House

David Wagoner

As a boy, I haunted an abandoned house
Whose basement was always full of dark-green water
Or dark-green ice in winter,
Where frogs came back to life and sang each spring.

On broken concrete under the skeleton
Of a roof, inside ribbed walls, I listened alone
Where the basement stairs went down
Under the water, down into their music.

During storms, our proper house would be flooded too.
The water would spout from drains, through the foundations
And climb the basement stairs
But silently, and would go away silently,

As silent as my mother and father were
All day and during dinner and after
And after the radio
With hardly a murmur all the way into sleep.

All winter, the frogs had slept in an icy bed,
Remembering how to sing when it melted.
If I made a sound, they stopped
And listened to me sing nothing, singing nothing.

But gradually, finally April would come pouring
Out of their green throats in a green chorus
To chorus me home toward silence.
Theirs was the only house that sang all night.

Breaking Through

Their basement is so quiet—my parents, pale, coming and going quickly, mysterious and without color. How do we find it, this second house—with color in the basement, the rich green water flooding this basement, the truth deep inside. Color—my pen finally has ink that I can see. I return to my parents, to my silent beginnings. I can sing now, sing their silences. They are the pale blank basement. I can hear their white voices. With my green water, my ink, I can return now and write them down. I can finally sing.

The Sounds of Silence

The other house was green with flood
or frozen ice
where frogs sang
on broken concrete,
a chorus of green
and abandon.
Sometimes our house, the proper house,
flooded too,
but it would go away
silently,
like the silence of my parents
in the proper house.
When spring came
so did the streams of green
through the broken concrete
and I alone would
go to the abandoned
other house where the frogs would stop
at the sound of my murmur—
and start again in their chorus of green.

Friends

My house is full
of silent people.
The abandoned house
is alive.
The abandoned house
is singing
with frogs.
The frogs fill me up.
The frogs listen
to me.

A Loud Silence

The only singing house
I hear is the house
I never go home to.
The songs of course are
silent, the strife, of course,
is strident.
What goes unsaid is
louder than what I
choose to hear,
louder than frozen frogs
croaking their way towards
their green April
and away from the silent house
that no longer hears my
voice.

In the basement of the old house,
a puddle of green water.
A frog jumps in.
Plop!

House or Home?

The house I call home is certainly not.
No one lives there but the frogs.
My house has ghosts living in it,
but I haunt my home,
scaring the frogs into
silence.
My house isn't scary.
The ghosts are very quiet.
They go to bed by ten.
My home is happy as long as
I am quiet.
The frogs sing and sing, but
I am quiet.

Silence and Sound

In spring,
after the ice melts
and the drains fill
the concrete cracks
of the basement floor
with green water,
the frogs are born
to keep me company
and fill my silent nights
with songs.

Green-Houses

Every house was the other house;
every house we borrowed was green.
Before our muddy cakes dried
my brothers and sister and mother
would be walking to greener
houses,
houses stained with others'
blood, not our own.
The homes we left behind were red.

Who would be the man of the house?
Who would introduce the newness,
the green doors, the green water
from the faucets, the green blades
of grass along the front gutters?
Where would our next house be?
What name should I use to introduce
myself at school?
Another green boy in a blue neighborhood.
When I left on mornings
I wondered if my mother
would stay where she stood.

What I Need

I need music
I need the sounds of music
I need to listen, listening, to have listened
to the sounds of music
In my proper house
in my proper silent house,
I am abandoned to silence.
Alone in silence
I listen
but hear hardly a murmur.
And so
I seek any chorus of pale green frogs
to sing all night
and drown silence in pale green water.

Dark and Proper

The other house was mine.
It was dark in winter,
but so was mine.
Mom and Dad, silent;
all I heard was silence,
dark silence, under the house,
in the house, dark and haunted.
Proper was silence in winter, spring
Other was silence in winter, life in spring.
April brought life to the other,
frogs singing all night.
April brought silence to my parents',
silence that haunted and haunted.

Quietly Quiet

I hear the silence of frogs sleeping
quiet
quietly sleeping...as steady a murmur
as my parents
sleeping... .
in their wake-ful hours.
Sleepwalking silently
through the morning
through the last humming radio play
through the dark night
and I lay quietly listening
to their silence.
I learned that way,
the way of silence, the way of sleep.
No wishful thinking green-croaking frog
come April a-croaking with
his rhythm
Maybe I should turn in
my skin
turn it green and wake up
with the spring
Ah, yes. A-croaking croaking
as surely
as my parents rose in silence.

> For some reason, in re-creations, images flow in and out of consciousness. Some stand out for me, and those are the ones I jot down.
>
> —Student

Comment: The images of the poem evoke such a profusion of images in the listener that there emerges a wild tangle of memories, sounds, tastes, touches, in the writer which catapult them into writing their Re-creation.

Narrative Similitude

In narrative similitude the heard *story* embedded in the the poem becomes primary and triggers in listeners who focus on the *story* pattern an analogous story from their own experience. So a poem about a daughter poised on the brink of pubescence may trigger a personal story about my own shift in awareness at that age.

In listening to someone else's story, which always contains a plot, a sequence of events, this event reminds us of some approximate event in our own lives. Ultimately, we all tell the same story of excitement or suffering or challenge or sadness or achievement or despair or transition. Only the details differ. Here is the story of a specific poet, a specific woman, a specific voice, who narrates her experience of a daughter's coming pubescence embedded in a haircut. The Re-creations below come from a group of English teachers in a workshop who were experimenting with the process themselves before going into their classrooms to try it on their own. These Re-creations take the universal story of the pain associated with cutting the umbilical cord and apply it where each re-creator's emotional connection was at that moment in their lives, from unborn child, to daughter-to-mother, to seventh-grader, to the young suitor once-removed from the fiercely protective mother.

The Possessive

My daughter, my son, which will it be?
This child which started from next to nothing
but is something growing inside me.
Its face is veiled from us now
but will appear and disclose itself.
This new carbon copy of me will cut through
and, like a soldier removing his helmet,
show itself—vulnerable to the world.

Seventh Grade HAIR

Hair!
It's mine and I can do anything
I please with it.
It's mine.
Its color is none of your business
and its shape is mine alone to shape!

He does my bidding.
I guide his keen blade
gently, gently
and precisely. The carbon steel
cuts away the frayed edges
mind-of-their-own cowlicks
and misbehaving wisps
until I am left satisfied
with what I see.

Shocked? Surprised? Gross, you say?
It's my message to you,
for now.

The Possessive

Sharon Olds

My daughter—as if I
owned her—that girl with the
hair wispy as a frayed bellpull

has been to the barber, that knife grinder,
and had the edge of her hair sharpened.

Each strand now cuts
both ways. The blade of new bangs
hangs over her red-brown eyes
like carbon steel.
All the little
spliced ropes are sliced. The curtain of
dark paper-cuts veils the face that
started from next to nothing in my body—

My body. My daughter. I'll have to find
another word. In her bright helmet
she looks at me as if across a
great distance. Distant fires can be
glimpsed in the resin light of her eyes:

the watch fires of an enemy, a while before
the war starts.

The Possessive

(For Tim)
You dare approach…
ENEMY
INTRUDER
INTERLOPER…
My daughter's first lover.
I, Goddess of the Arcadian ranch-style,
despise you.
Affable youth,
smiling ingratiatingly,
laughing too heartily.
I spurn your diffident attempts to
distract me,
disarm me,
purchase my grudging approval with
sugary offerings,
floral oblations,
white-cartoned fatted calf from a Chinese restaurant,
sacrifices
to appease the wrath of this ever-vigilant Artemis,
sentry at the vestibule or in the backyard cemented forest.

OH, T-SHIRTED WARRIOR,
YOU HAVE RAVISHED THE VIRGIN PRINCESS
AND SO, I DECREE, YOU MUST DIE!
SHALL I PEPPER THAT TAUT CHEST WITH ARROWS
OR TEAR OUT YOUR ENTRAILS AND
RITUALLY COIL THEM AROUND
THE PROUD BULGE?

Are you blind to the sacrifice you wrest from me?
Her skin, the essence of which obsesses, addicts you,
came from my body.
Observe her berylline eyes
and then mine.
Young man, you rob me!

But I, more wise crone than fiery, vengeful goddess,
must allow the plunder,
must remember
another young hero
whose urgent kisses clamped lush, swollen lips,
whose comfortable weight
cleaved my body,
fashioning that tender fledgling,
now grown full-female.

I watch the youthful replica of my own visage
turn from my eyes, which once summed up her universe,
to meet yours.

—Nancy Wambach

Possession

The Achtung
the Sonic Boom
the Big Bang
of warmongers,
mother and daughter,
grinding knives
knocking helmets
lighting fires.

Mommy: Let's sit before the fire,
share the peace pipe,
brush each others' fraying hair,
promise peace.

— Kate Evans

What We Have Learned in this Chapter:

Narrative, idea, sound, and feeling similitude nudges otherwise non-linear, erratic experiences toward a gist, a focus of some sort.

Like particle, field, and wave, a work of art is simultaneously process and product. In the sense of process, the heard work becomes fluid, like juggler's balls, held aloft by the spoken medium of the poet's language. Active listeners regroup the balls, participants, into their own configuration of meaning, thus also become creators. As long as human beings are creative, they transcend whatever has been and IS to articulate their own vision and their own time-without obliterating the past or that which has already been done. A Re-creation is a way of BUILDING on what has gone before. It's a way of re-cognizing, of knowing again— and in a deep way— what has gone before.

C·H·A·P·T·E·R·S·E·V·E·N

To Imitate or Not to Imitate

BORROWING VS. SYNTHESIS

T.S. Eliot, who wrote some of the most famous poems of the early twentieth century, argued that the creative self relies on what has gone before, that the individual mind can only draw from its creative predecessors. He uses as an example one of the great writers of all time, Shakespeare. Shakespeare built on the Roman Plutarch's *Lives* for plays like *Julius Caesar*, on *Holinshed's Chronicles* for plays like *Henry the Fourth*, and on a predecessor, *Thomas Kidd*, for *Hamlet*. He used the traditional stories and histories and plots but transformed their elements into dynamic images, ideas, feelings, voices—in short, into new coherences, new patterns of meaning—which have become unforgettable and which still speak to us 500 years later. In re-creating Holinshed, Plutarch, and Kidd, he not only generated his own images, ideas feelings, language, voice, but some of the greatest, most quoted lines in human history. The plot of *Hamlet* may have been from Thomas Kidd, but "To be or not to be that is the question" was not. The plot of *Julius Caesar* may have come from Plutarch, but the line. "I come to bury Caesar, not to praise him," was not. The plot of *Macbeth* may have been from Holinshed, but "Tomorrow and tomorrow and tomorrow/creeps in this petty pace from day to day/to the last syllable of recorded time" is not.

> Was Du ererbt von deinen Vaetern hast, erwirb es um es zu besitzen.
>
> —Johann Wolfgang von Goethe
>
> *(What you inherited from your fathers, you must earn to own.)*

The lesson to be learned from Shakespeare is his recognition of the past's stories and wisdoms and knowing them again by recasts it in a new shape, into new expressions of meaning. This literary borrowing process flies in the face of every nineteenth and twentieth century idea of creative exclusiveness, the idea that only a few geniuses can be creative. All human beings move in the luminous medium of a living tradition, of a life-stream; we all have the potential to transform the given, the traditional, the known—into the tentative, hesitant, risking, uncertain flight of new expression.

> What moves men of genius, or rather, what inspires their work, is not new ideas, but their obsession with the idea that what has already been said is still not enough.
>
> —Eugene Delacroix

Life itself is a creative force, adapting to changes. Margaret Wheatley points out that because life is dynamic, it "delights in our explorations; and, when we stop imposing rules and tests, and limits… we grow into greater capacity." The more we quantify and codify and bureaucratize, the more we impose increasingly unnatural boundaries on learners, making them believe they can only be observers or, at best, participants in the great flow of knowledge, but not creators. In fact, inquisitive and creative human nature is built by what Loren Eiseley called "the invisible pyramid of individuals on which civilization is built." All human knowing is a bricolage of what came before.

Throughout recorded history, human beings have incorporated and transcended old discoveries to make new ones. For example, between 800 and 900 A.D. the Chinese used engraved wooden blocks to print books. This process became the basis for the invention of the Gutenberg Printing Press with movable metal parts. Where would most cultures be without borrowing, adaptation, derivation? Sir Isaac Newton, who took credit in 1678 for explaining the laws of planetary motion, probably drew on the work of Robert Hooke, as well as others.

He acknowledged his debt with his famous statement: "If I have seen farther it is by standing on the shoulders of giants." Einstein traded, built, scaffolded, interlinked, bricolaged, ensembled his ideas, and, in doing so, created a new synthesis. On a recent show on the most influential people of the millennium, Gutenberg was chosen as number one because his invention had shaped so many of the other people on the list. Without him, they said, we probably wouldn't know Shakespeare, Darwin, Einstein.

British artist Michael Ayrton argued that "we are dominated by romantic notions which have raised the virtue of originality so high that to imitate has become one of the artist's capital crimes, an activity suited only to young students who blush to be accused of it." He continues, "The general prejudice against the copy today lies not only in our faith in mechanical techniques [of photography] but also in the irrational belief that copying verges on forgery." Ayrton tells the story of the fourteen year-old Michelangelo who copied Giotto, of Rubens who copied Michelangelo and many other artists who became famous in their own right. He concludes that "the artist is, and always has been, involved with existing images, whether ephemeral or not" and that such translation or Re-creation is part of the process of discovering and clarifying his own experience.

Professor James R. Kincaid in a recent *New Yorker* article refers to a story about Helen Keller who was once accused of plagiarism, to which she responded, "it is certain that I cannot always distinguish my own thoughts from those I read, because what I read becomes the very substance of my mind." Kincaid argues, "copying, or imitating, is vital to gaining initial entry into a discourse." A professor and poet who had his work plagiarized, Kincaid concludes, "pure *originality* is an over-the-rainbow idea; none of us invent the language we employ, our education, our culture, or our history." He concludes that the concept of originality is "relative and exists on a scale." Ruminating about our "grim clutch on purist ideas of originality," Kincaid invents *the plagiarism proctor* who "... is sickened by the idea that he might invite other voices in... . His vision often seems to reach no further than secured tidiness: a padlocked library, with every word in its place, dusted, and correctly filed."

Re-creations as Metaphorms:

Todd Siler, director of Psi-Phi Communications and interested in the arts' interaction with science and technology, calls such interaction a metaphorming process. Similarly, transpersonal psychologist Ken Wilber talks about the human mind's on-going "transcending that which we incorporate." The famed English professor Northrop Frye insisted that "poetry can only be made out of other poems; novels out of other novels...." that "we, like poems, come into being within structures already in place."

> When I begin a picture, there is somebody who works with me. Toward the end, I get the impression that I have been working alone—without a collaborator.
>
> —Picasso

I noted the process of metaphorming over and over again in my own children as they were growing and mimicking and learning. Take for example, my youngest, Simone. When she was seven, I found some scribbled writing entitled *The Dark Is Rising.* Puzzled because I couldn't imagine how a seven-year-old could come up with such an un-seven year-old sentence, I found the answer shortly after: Her two older sisters had been reading a novel for adolescents by Susan Cooper entitled, *The Dark is Rising.* Those words on the cover of a book became the lightning flash which triggered the impulse to articulate what this seven year-old felt/heard/saw/imaged: a floating earth half bathed in light gradually overtaken by darkness covering first this and that, then—an amazing intuitive grasp: "and everything is pertected by the sun." This child, for herself, grasped in words the cyclical nature of light and dark, very likely BECAUSE of a title she had read, *The Dark Is Rising.* The sentence, created by another, was so evocative to her, she felt the need to EX-press what it meant to her in words.

Transcending and Incorporating

We transcend what has gone before, but when we are truly learning we incorporate some aspect of it. Visual artists have a long and honorable tradition of building on others' work, including the great twentieth century innovator, Pablo Picasso. Just by making a list of a handful of his many statements during his long creative life, one can see that he gave credit where credit was due, however obliquely:

"As if I didn't know Cezanne! He was my one and only master! Don't you think I looked at his pictures? I spent years studying them. Cezanne! It was the same with all of us—he was like our father."
(in Brassai, 1966)

Velasquez left us his idea of the people of his epoch. Undoubtedly they were different from what he painted them, but we cannot conceive a Philip IV in any other way than the one Velasquez painted."
(in De Zayas, 1923)

I'd give the whole of Italian painting for Vermeer of Delft. There's a painter who simply said what he had to say without bothering about anything else. None of those mementos of antiquity for him."
(Letter, 1936)

What I really like about [El Greco) are his portraits, these gentlemen with their pointed beards."
(in Kahnweiler, 1955)

Figure 7-1

Figure 7-2

Vermeer, Cezanne, Velasquez, El Greco, however disparate their styles, all became part of Picasso's astonishing growth through being incorporated in the artist's ever-expanding aesthetic world map.

The Gradient Inherent in Re-creation

Transpersonal psychologist Ken Wilber's phrase, that we *transcend AND incorporate*, is absolutely fitting here. Simone *transcended* Cooper's title by writing her piece, but she *incorporated* the title—she hadn't even read the book—probably the title startled her into an emotional connection, it became an affect-link, and she transformed it into her seven-year-old's world vision of what the rising dark meant to her. As Tobias Wolff says so beautifully, the mind does not claim language but is claimed by it "as if it were another parent."

Just as children are claimed by the language they hear and read, enabling them to grow beyond where they are now, so Picasso's borrowing is really a way of knowing the multiple ways of interpreting the visual world. What he synthesizes becomes part of him in the very act of making his own imaginary worlds visible.

> Language is our meeting place, the sea we all live in. When I watched my children learning to talk, I had the sense that they were not so much learning language as being claimed by it, taken into its arms as if it were another parent, and so it is.
>
> —Tobias Wolff

> If you search into the question of knowledge, you will find the only things you can be said truly to understand are those you have made yourself.
>
> —Giambattista Vico

Metaphorming Metaphorms:

Robert Frost's famous poem, *Nothing Gold Can Stay* has been memorized by many and read by many more. Clearly, Frost's poem, both in form and content, served as a powerful affect-link for Linda Pastan's creation, *Posterity*:

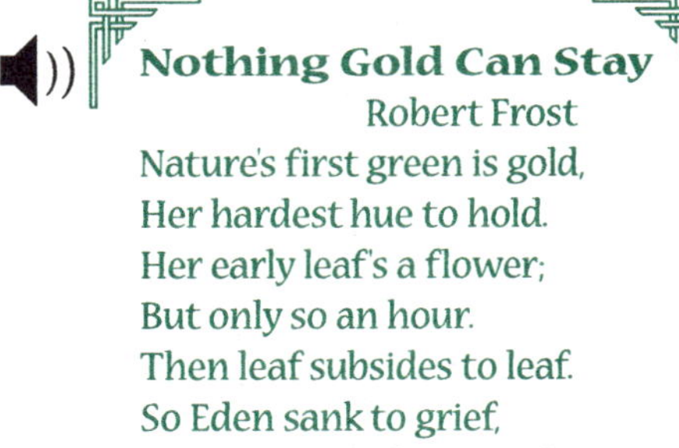

Nothing Gold Can Stay
Robert Frost
Nature's first green is gold,
Her hardest hue to hold.
Her early leaf's a flower;
But only so an hour.
Then leaf subsides to leaf.
So Eden sank to grief,
So dawn goes down to day.
Nothing gold can stay.

Posterity
Linda Pastan
For every newborn child
We planted one live tree,
A green posterity,
So death could be beguiled
By root and branch and flower
To abdicate some power.
And we were reconciled

Now we must move away
Leaving the trees behind
For anyone to climb.
The gold-rimmed sky goes gray.
Snow, as we turn our backs
Obliterates our tracks.
Not even leaves can stay.

Cycle

Not even
leaves can
stay. In
the river
of wind
that pulls
the fragile
green from
the branch
to float
flat-veined
in the dance
of the wind,
to crumble
with the crunch
of death into dust
to be born
beneath the soil again—
Not even leaves
can stay.

Fascinated by the linking of these two creative expressions, I read both Frost's poem and Pastan's poem to a group of students to see how they would listen, what they would process, and how they would incorporate—or keep separate—the two voices. Students heard them each twice, then re-created them without any directions regarding the fact that these were two separate poems by different writers:

Going Out with a Bang

I think about it sometimes. Should I be burned or buried when I die? I've always thought a Viking funeral would be cool, longboat and all. But then I think about all the bacteria and worms which would go hungry if I didn't leave my body to them. Ironic that all life lives on death. Bacteria feed on me, trees feed on bacteria, and we feed on trees. Not a food chain, but a circle. I'm gonna go with the Viking funeral.

In time I came across other metaphorms, some using the original as a diving platform, other times staying close to the original sound and sense, yet expressing its own version of the *story*.

Men at Forty

Donald Justice

Men at forty
Learn to close softly
The doors to rooms they will not be
Coming back to.

At rest on a stair landing,
They feel it
Moving beneath them now like the deck of a ship,
Though the swell is gentle.

And deep in mirrors
They rediscover
The face of the boy as he practices tying
His father's tie there in secret

And the face of that father,
Still warm with the mystery of lather.
They are more fathers than sons themselves now.
Something is filling them, something

That is like the twilight sound
Of the crickets, immense,
Filling the woods at the foot of the slope
Behind their mortgaged houses.

Women at Thirty
Maurya Simon

Women at thirty
Learn to swing slightly
In the hinges of their steps
As they ascend.

At ease on the carpeting
They feel it gliding
Beneath them now like an air-borne sail,
Though its speed is slowed down.

And deep in mirrors
They recover
The face of the girl as she tries on
Her mother's smile and kisses

The face of that mother
Still warmed by the mystery of father.
They are more and more like women now.
Something is touching them, something

That is like the sun's brush
Of white light, minute,
Unfurling the ferns at the base of the yard
Beyond their children's windows.

The Gradient of Metaphorms:

Of all the metaphorms that resulted from my experiments with Re-creations, I found that the most derivative came from Mary Oliver's beautiful life manifesto, *When Death Comes.* I was puzzled for a long time, using the poem several times to see if different things would happen, and almost always the Re-creations used several phrases from Oliver's poem, despite the fact that the poem was relatively long. I finally realized that the most-used phrases produced images so strong that they acted as attractors for most listeners…phrases such as "hungry bear in autumn," "snaps my purse shut," "iceberg between the shoulder blades," and especially, the clause, "When death comes…"

When Death Comes

Mary Oliver

When death comes
like the hungry bear in autumn;
when death comes and takes all the bright coins from his purse

to buy me, and snaps the purse shut;
when death comes
like the measle-pox;

when death comes
like an iceberg between the shoulder blades,

I want to step through the door full of curiosity, wondering;
what is it going to be like, that cottage of darkness?

And therefore I look upon everything
as a brotherhood and a sisterhood,
and I look upon time as no more than an idea,
and I consider eternity as another possibility,

and I think of each life as a flower, as common
as a field daisy, and as singular,

and each name a comfortable music in the mouth
tending, as all music does, toward silence,

and each body a lion of courage, and something
precious to the earth.

When it's over, I want to say all my life
I was a bride married to amazement;
I was the bridegroom taking the world into my arms.

When it's over, I don't want to wonder
if I have made of my life something particular, and real.
I don't want to find myself sighing and frightened,
or full of argument.

I don't want to end up simply having visited this world.

When I Go

When I go on to the next life,
I want to be a pet of mine.
I put in my request now because
my pets have the best life.
They play, they jump, they sniff,
they eat, they howl, they run,
they sleep, they curl up
in little balls and get
petted and petted and petted
and loved with a capital L
When they limp, they get picked up
and when they cry, they get stroked
and touched.
And when they poop, they even get
congratulated.

When Death Comes

While the tide of life runs high,
I will devote my days to another horizon,
not hungry pain
or icy coins,
not awaiting the abode of darkness,
but seeing there, in death's approach,
a light—it can be here
if only I will open my eyes.
Is this a visit?
Or is this a journey
through time's meaninglessness
into the day after
when all is made clear,
made right
and understandable.
A veil of amazement
is the visit of death,
an unwanted visitor
never successfully deferred.

Just Visiting

I hope to welcome death,
stepping through its door
through the cottage of darkness, just for a moment,
then into the light.
I see death as I do a flower,
common— we must all go to it—
yet singular, each departure unique from the next.
When I leave, I want to know
that amazement was my bridegroom,
to seek amazement till death do us part—
because I realize now that I'm just visiting.

Cosmic

When death comes, it won't be anything like
we think it will be.
There will be no rigor mortis, stiffening us
and no one tossing piles of dirt on top of us,
six feet under.
No big deal to die, really.
It's just transforming from one thing into something.
No more 2 legs, 2 arms, 2 everything else,
Just one. One's enough. One what?
I don't know. Someday we'll all know,
but we won't care so much,
& there will be one of all of us,
everything shared.
Cosmic, huh?

When Death Comes

When death comes, I will be a hungry bear
I'm full of curiosity,
looking for that cottage of darkness
with all of my secrets inside.
Life is not a flower,
nor music in my mouth.
I'm full of curiosity
searching for the answers.

When Death Comes

When one dies, where does he go?
Where does life go when there is death?
Does time keep going, or does time stop?
When one dies...

When one dies, can it be felt?
Where does death come from?
Can one speak with death?
When one dies, are all answers there?

When one dies, do they have to
live underground forever?
Time must never end, so where does one go
when they die?

When Death Comes

Like Autumn, Death comes with a chill,
an iceberg between the shoulder blades.
Death will buy me with bright coins,
but I shall not segue;
I shall not sigh,
for life is like a song that ends in silence.
In my life, I was not merely a visitor,
but a participant,
seeing life with amazement and curiosity,
holding the world in my arms like a bridegroom.
When death comes, I will walk through that door,
as I once walked through it before
to behold
this life.

Comment: The gradient of transcending and incorporating is clearly shown in the Re-creations of Oliver's poem. The images were so strong that several re-creators used one or more as the diving board from which to write their own piece. This led to a spirited discussion of the difference between a Re-creation, a copy, an imitation, and plagiarism. Students decided that, if they would follow through on a class publication, they would do one of two things: 1) Either revise their Re-creation by adapting Oliver's exact words or 2) subtitle their Re-creation (after Oliver).

The Noun Sandwich:

I continued to experiment with the idea of metaphorms. One day I came across a poem by American poet Stanley Kunitz, the metaphorm of a poem by the Russian poet Aleksandr Blok. Although I don't read Russian, Kunitz' poem is very likely a loose translation of Blok:

The Scene
(after Aleksandr Blok)
Stanley Kunitz,

Night. Street. Lamp. Drugstore.
A world of dim and sleazy light.
You may live twenty five years more.
Nothing will change. No way out.

You die. You're born again and all
Will be repeated as before:
The cold ripple of a canal.
Night. Street. Lamp. Drugstore.

I asked students to metaphorm Kunitz' metaphorm by making a *noun sandwich* by clustering only nouns around the noun *(The) Scene.* Of the clustered noun associations, they would select the four which spoke to them most directly. From these they would form the two identical slices of bread, so to speak, then fill it with whatever those nouns dictated.

Here are some of the resulting metaphorms:

The Growing Scene
Skyline. Park. Lake. Lions.
Taking the El into the Loop,
studying in the old library on Randolph,
Dust. Latin letters. The Art Institute.
The books, the paintings my home lacked,
drawn to images that would matter,
finding them, all on my own.
How did I know to do that?
Skyline. Park. Lake. Lions.
Dawn Chase

The Learning Scene
Desk. Chair. Blackboard. Classroom.
Green walls cast drabness over warm bodies.
Teacher. Students. Lessons. Learning.
After twenty five years or so you finish,
then graduate, only to begin again.
Desk. Chair. Blackboard. Classroom.
Mary Bowers

Coming Back

The dark porch
belongs to my old house.
Mother prays for us.
She is afraid our
lessons won't stick.
Strings of beads,
the Rosary lessons we learned,
remind us
of our simple, old life,
and we return
again.

On the Move

The house full of mothers,
full of Virgin Marys
always makes me want to stop.
But I can't stop, can't stop.
I must always move on,
must keep up with society,
must progress, progress, progress.
I always have to say no,
say no to simplicity,
say no to the old Adobe house,
say no to umbilical cords.

La Casa

Rosemary Catacalos

The house by the acequia
its front porch dark and
cool with begonias,
an old house, always there,
always of the same adobe,
always full of the same lessons.
We would like to stop.
We know we belonged there once.
Our mothers are inside.
All the mothers are inside,
lighting candles, swaying
back and forth on their knees,
begging The Virgin's forgiveness
for having reeled us out
on such very weak string.
They are afraid for us.
They know we will not stop.
We will only wave as we pass by.
They will go on praying
that we might be simple again.

Explosion

In the sanctuary
the mothers pray for our simplicity.
They fear we will never come back where we belong.
But we do not want their forgiveness.
So we smile and leave them to their candles.
We light spark plugs, so we can move away.
Spark plugs have more potential energy than candles

You Can't Go Home Again

The coolness of home beckons.
The mothers, the mothers who fear—
their lives go unchanged.
We pass the Adobe. We hear the prayers,
soft, rhythmical.
Always they pray for the same.
Always their prayers go unanswered.
The Virgin is with them. She is the mother
and the daughter,
the life,
the salvation.
Coolness beckons but loses our souls.
Weep not mother.
We are well.

One House, Many Houses

This house, that house, fragrant with begonias,
cool, dark, filled with life and death
and memories.
This house, that house, many houses
filled with candles and praying mothers and swaying.
Lessons in adobe or brick or girders to the sky,
Virgins forgiving us sinners.
Waving, praying, sampling, playing
Those same old lessons again, once again,
on our knees
in this house, that house, many houses.

Comment: Catacalos' poem, too, generated more Re-creations that resembled the original than many other poems, especially in *voice*. My guess is that the home/house image in the context of the adolescent cutting of the umbilical cord resonated deeply in the listeners, most of whom were just past adolescence. *Coming Back* speaks of returning to the hearth and to the family. *You Can't Go Home Again* focuses on a loss of spirituality. *One House, Many Houses* heightens awareness of the cyclical nature of departure and return. *Explosion* hints at the power of the automobile to win freedom from low-wattage candles. *On the Move* implies that a fast-paced culture of progress and hurry-sickness precludes return.

Conclusion:

Any Re-creation refers both backward and forward along a gradient. At one extreme of the spectrum, the Re-creator uses the original only as a springboard for her own expression of an analogical—hence highly metaphorical—leap to personal experience. The attractor is the emotional similitude which startled the writer into her own meditation/piece. In mid-gradient, words and phrases from the original build a bridge between original and Re-creation. At the other extreme, there is a close resemblance between original and Re-creation. Yet, despite the resemblance, the mind will create its own pattern of meaning—even when a number of the words and phrases are used. It is not plagiarism because the heard piece is reconstructed from memory, not from a text before the writer. The created artifact is filtered through the experiential sieve of each mind—only to be transformed into something different as the unique expression of the hearer who then DOES something with the listening, metaphorms the heard piece into his own expression. A Re-creation is not a paraphrase; it is not a copy; it is not plagiarized, nor is it mere imitation. As a metaphorm it is its own configuration, a melody of resonances.

C·H·A·P·T·E·R·E·I·G·H·T

Short or Long?

COMPRESSION OR EXPANSION

A Re-creation may be highly compressed or expanded, depending on the rapid flow of ideas or economy of expression. Some writers manage almost a page in three minutes. Some write only four lines. Both brevity and length have advantages. Long or short, we can test the boundaries of language—and of our minds—by telescoping or expanding with a rich overlay of associations to take us beyond the most obvious way to say it, since we are guided by the poem just heard. Sometimes we are surprised into leaping over the most efficient way of saying something because the internal sense of flow urges us on to write until the last second before bringing closure. Sometimes we syncopate like a jazz musician, hearing echoes of the original melody broken up and returning in snatches. Often, these become the shorter Re-creations. Thus, Re-creations beget amazing variability....Let's look at a long poem (forty-eight lines) which engendered six lines as the shortest, to eighteen lines as the longest, in three minutes. Among the things I discovered is: that longer is not necessarily better, and shorter is it necessarily worse.

Proofreading

Philip Dacey

There is no way to know
you have them all.
Who is going to say
there is no snake in the grass
just because you can't see it?
So you mow down the grass—so what does that prove?
It proves that now there's a clearing
surrounded by grass. The grass goes on
and on. Love the grass
and what is
or is not in it.

If you're proofing your life,
you're weeding while reading.
Is it clean now? Remember
the Navajo weaver left a flaw
in the pattern, a loose thread, a tongue
to tickle the air, arouse it, so the god
of the air and all else would not be offended
by presumptuous perfection. Uppity.
Fire for the gods:
for men, typos.

There is
a snake in the grass
and his name is Desire.
Gold diamonds ride in file
his back, nor defile
him or his seat
of honor, our hearts,
heartland, grassland,
great plains like a sentence
stretching from here to there,
brushfires like commas
burning themselves up,
old buildings collapsing
like an object into its predicate,
a kiss into a gesture
of betrayal, a coming that is a going.

Someone somewhere has his fingers in the tray of type.
Praise him, curse him,
but let the curse appear as
a course, a way,
and the praise as
praise, the mistake in the manuscript
that gets repeated in the final product,
book, breath,
and thereby, Proofreader,
becomes correct.

Snake-in-Waiting

In my computer
hides the snake
coiled and waiting.
His flicking tongue
kisses my fingers,
causing errors,
to his delight.
Gold diamonds dance
behind the flirting cursor.
Mistakes arise, and
I fire off curses.
If only there weren't a
snake coiled inside
my electronic apple!

Improvement

The fields, wild with grasses,
flourish in their imperfections.
The golden snake is human desire,
slithering in and out of the weeds.
Its command: improvement.
And so we mow the grasses down,
and this new clearing—is this perfection?
Then what of the long grasses?
The nested field mouse?
The hawk?

The Snake Named Desire

There is a snake in the grass,
and his name is Desire,
slithering, snaking, winding himself
around our lives
making us search out perfection.
But oh, how presumptuous
perfection is: The Navajos,
wise ones, left tiny flaws
in their work—their pottery,
weavings, rings,
knowing perfection is not human
and being human is not perfection.
No, perfection does not exist,
but while that snake
lies hidden in the grass—
that snake named Desire—
perfection is what we seek.

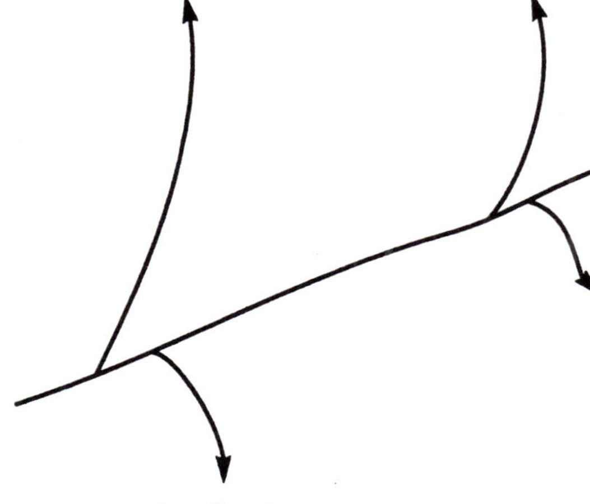

It's My Life

It is my life,
a heartland stretching
full of love of what is
or is not in it.
My life goes on
and on
and on
woven perfectly.
Yes. Woven perfectly.
Yes, there are flaws,
mistakes I'd like to fix
but once they've taken form,
been printed in my history,
they've become a part of me,
my breath, my being, my Self.

Perfection

It goes on and on...
Is it... or is it not...?
Does it offend?
Will it end?
A kiss, a gesture, a desire:
the heartland shifts and changes,
wanting to have it all
precise—and not a flaw.

Comment: Because of the brevity of time allotted for the writing, I examined the Re-creations for complexity and saw that a short piece might easily be as complex or sophisticated as a longer piece. I saw also that, knowing the limited time frame ahead of time, writers simply wrote until they sensed completion.

Re-creations of a Passage of Fiction:

Since I rarely, if ever, encountered a Re-creation that was not a self-contained *whole*, I wondered whether it was the nature of the compression of the poetic as opposed to the expansion of prose that played a role in such consistent completion. As a result, I began to experiment with fiction. What would happen, I wondered, if I asked students to re-create only a piece, only one lonely passage, from a short story or even an entire novel? Would it make a difference if they knew they were listening to only a part of the whole? To find out, I chose a passage from James Joyce's short story, *Araby*.

The Magic of Dusk

We played in
the cold, short winter evenings
colored violet with dusk.
We made a career
of playing long in
the streets
and alleys with shadows,
our bodies small and cold
and glowing
In the street the lamps
lined up,
illuminated
a playmate's sister strolling
towards us,
sister— soft
smooth hair,
swinging skirt.
Magic

Twilight's Wild Moment

My favorite time of day was twilight, when there is light, but no heat. Everything dims to a purple blue, the raw colors of reflected sunlight. Then, we children, liberated from our evening meals, would run down the streets, our sounds excited by the approach of night. Parents would sit on porches, just within the yellow glow from inside, and settle their news in the calm of the summer evening. There could be no television or newspaper story as interesting as the singing of the cicadas in the growing dark. At last, we would run home, the cool evening air making our sweat sting on our cheeks. We had been wild one last time before the eternal captivity of brushing our teeth and slouching to bed.

-from **Araby**
James Joyce

When the short days of winter came dusk fell before we had well eaten our dinner. When we met in the street the houses had grown somber. The space of sky above us was the color of ever-changing violet and toward it the lamps of the street lifted their feeble lanterns. The cold air stung us and we played till our bodies glowed. Our shouts echoed in the silent street. The career of our play brought us through the dark muddy lanes behind the houses where we ran the gauntlet of the rough tribes from the cottages, to the back doors of the dark dripping gardens where odors arose from the ashpits, to the dark odorous stables where a coachman smoothed and combed the horse or shook music from the buckled harness. If my uncle was seen turning the corner we hid in the shadow until we had seen him safely housed. Or if Mangan's sister came out on the doorstep to call her brother in to his tea we watched her from our shadow peer up and down the street. We waited to see whether she would remain or go in and, if she remained, we left our shadow and walked to to Mangan's steps resignedly. She was waiting for us, her figure defined by the light from the half-opened door. Her brother always teased her before he obeyed and I stood by the railings looking at her. Her dress swung as she moved her body, and the soft rope of her hair tossed from side to side.

Evening Play

Evening play,
free play,
darkness providing the perfect setting for
hide-and-seek,
a game for all of us,
whose joy comes from startling.
The sheer pleasure of being startled!
A game for small ones and big ones,
teenagers looking for ways to connect.
What a wonderful evening.
Evening play.

Holding Hands

School
home
hands
Walking home hand in hand with Susie Williams
my hands sweat I am nervous thrilled excited the
creek has a levy which we use as a path toward
home It gets dark Hands We hold hands Love
there here We hide in shadows we pass behind
houses and mothers cook dinners and call in their
children Susie goes home we don't kiss we're not
ready for that yet maybe someday we will be
ready
dark
love
hands

When I was eight I would play until the night came on, the dusk slipping over the world quietly enclosed at first in the sky above our heads, between the buildings. As the violet glowed stronger, the world would suddenly, for a flash, have sharp outlines, shapes of heavy black cut out against the coming night. I would be running often, running hard. I would miss that moment, but then there were the times after the shouts had flown past me down the streets, when the echoes of my feet clacked by underneath me, and then I would pull up breathless at the front steps. My throat raw, the air over and past. Mangin's sister there, in the dim, three years older, her long hair, her rich brown rope dangling heavy and warm. I would stop running to watch, sometimes from the shadows, feel her glow coming on, when I was eight. I watched the night come on. I felt its chill, I felt its warmth, when I was eight I fell in love.

In late autumn, in the hours before dusk, we'd play football in the street. Wrapped in sweatshirts to keep out the biting air, we'd run back and forth between the glow of the lamp posts. Dreams we made, lived, those nights—today a quarterback, tomorrow a receiver, always a star. When the moon and stars finally showed up against the black night, we would retreat to our prospective doors, to the smell of homemade soup and dark bread.

Comment: I was elated. As with poems, the process elicited marvelous language rhythms, narratives, images. Furthermore, the division between the resulting prose and poetic forms was about even. If students could write so exquisitely from a single passage of a whole story, what would happen if I read an entire short story just once instead of twice, then gave them three minutes to re-create it in whatever way presented itself. They certainly didn't have time to worry about what they might do or could do or would do if they understood it better. I selected a two-page short story, reading it only once, which meant they both listened and clustered words and phrases around a blank center.

Re-Creating an Entire Short Story

Yours

Mary Robison

Allison struggled away from her white Renault, limping with the weight of the last of the pumpkins. She found Clark in the twilight on the twig-and-leaf-littered porch behind the house. He wore a wool shawl. He was moving up and back in a padded glider, pushed by the ball of his slippered foot.

Allison lowered a big pumpkin, let it rest on the wide floorboards.

Clark was much older—seventy-eight to Allison's thirty-five. They were married. They were both quite tall and looked something alike in their facial features. Allison wore a natural-hair wig. It was a thick blond hood around her face. She was dressed in bright-dyed denims today. She wore durable clothes, usually, for she volunteered afternoons at a children's daycare center.

She put one of the smaller pumpkins on Clark's long lap. "Now, nothing surreal," she told him. "Carve just a regular face. These are for kids."

In the foyer, on the Hepplewhite desk, Allison found the maid's chore list with its cross-offs, which included Clark's supper. Allison went quickly through the day's mail: a garish coupon packet, a bill from Jamestown Liquors, November's pay-TV program guide, and the worst thing, the funniest, an already opened, extremely unkind letter from Clark's relations up North. "You're an old fool," Allison read, and, "You're being cruelly deceived." There was a gift check for Clark enclosed, but it was uncashable, signed, as it was, "Jesus H. Christ."

Late, late into this night, Allison and Clark gutted and carved the pumpkins together, at an old table set on the back porch, over newspaper after soggy newspaper, with paring knives and with spoons and with a Swiss Army knife Clark used for exact shaping of tooth and eye and nostril. Clark had been a doctor, an internist, but also a Sunday watercolorist. His four pumpkins were expressive and artful. Their carved features were suited to the sizes and shapes of the pumpkins. Two looked ferocious and jagged. One registered surprise. The last was serene and beaming.

Allison's four faces were less deftly drawn, with slits and areas of distortion. She had cut triangles for noses and eyes. The mouths she had made were just wedges—two turned up and two turned down.

By one in the morning they were finished. Clark, who had bent his long torso forward to work, moved back over to the glider and looked out sleepily at nothing. All the lights were out across the ravine.

Clark stayed. For the season and time, the Virginia night was warm. Most leaves had been blown away already, and the trees stood unbothered. The moon was round above them.

Allison cleaned up the mess.

"Your jack o'lanterns are much, much better than mine," Clark said to her.

"Like hell," Allison said.

"Look at me," Clark said, and Allison did.

She was holding a squishy bundle of newspapers. The papers reeked sweetly with the smell of pumpkin guts.

"Yours are far better," he said.

"You're wrong. You'll see when they're lit," Allison said.

She went inside, came back with yellow vigil candles. It took her a while to get each candle settled, and then to line up the results in a row on the porch railing. She went along and lit each candle and fixed the pumpkin lids over the little flames.

"See?" she said.

They sat together a moment and looked at the orange faces.

"We're exhausted. It's good night time," Allison said. "Don't blow out the candles. I'll put in new ones tomorrow."

That night, in their bedroom, a few weeks earlier in her life than had been predicted, Allison began to die. "Don't look at me if my wig comes off," she told Clark. "Please."

Her pulse cords were fluttering under his fingers. She raised her knees and kicked away the comforter. She said something to Clark about the garage being locked.

At the telephone, Clark had a clear view out back and down to the porch. He wanted to get drunk with his wife once more. He wanted to tell her, from the greater perspective he had, that to own only a little talent, like his, was an awful, plaguing thing; that being only a little special meant you expected too much, most of the time, and liked yourself too little. He wanted to assure her that she had missed nothing.

He was speaking into the phone now. He watched the jack-o-lanterns. The jack-o-lanterns watched him.

Snatches

Sweet-smelling pumpkin guts.
The lights were out across the ravine
the moon was round above them,
the carving knife lying on the porch
reflected the moon in its wet blade.
An old man wanting to get drunk,
a woman with a yellow mop for hair,
letters read, snatches of conversation,
the faces of the pumpkins gleaming in the night,
the old man watched the jack o' lanterns.
The jack o' lanterns watched him.

The Story... Continued

The pumpkin faces cast an eerie glow across the back porch. He sat there in the glider sliding back and forth. A year ago they argued her pumpkins were better. The air was cold and clear. He could hear the rattling bags of children climbing the steps. He made them come over and dropped a quarter in each bag. That's when he noticed the wig, the blond wig. On the porch. He didn't know how it got there. It smelled like her.

May/December

Their May-December romance is ending. Carving pumpkins, they are sharing each others' time. They could be watching TV instead, but they choose to carve pumpkins at this time of the year until Allison's final exit. How fitting that their last project, the Jack-o-Lanterns, are watching at the end.

Hooded and ferocious, death carved
itself into the sweet orange night,
its jagged slits and wedges cut into the
white clay moon.
I thought there was beauty in death
where leaves blow clean and soft
but it is a cruel gift.

Challenge

Expectation
and limitation:
One meets the other,
neither is the same;
a challenge issued—
given a name.

And to find two
for which expectation gives way to revelation
early or late in life—
still their import
a source of comfort

And to communicate
what one evaluates
and finds of greatest worth
that which weathers well
and if only to tell
as much as one knows
hoping the other grows
as did the first

And to watch ideas burst
and burn on bright
as Jack-o'Lanterns
on Hallowe'en night.

An although all flames
are later extinguished—
To have said all one wished.

The Dead and the Dying

It is the marriage of the dead to the dying. They carve their pumpkins one last night, scooping webs and seeds onto yesterday's newspaper. They take special care to shape the eyes, the mouth, the nostrils. This tooth's jagged, that one's smooth. They use their knives like doctors or sculptors. Finished, they have two heads, one surprised, one serene and beaming. Yellow flames shine faces on the wall. The morning wakes to soggy newspapers reeking of pumpkin guts, only one candle left burning.

Yours
Mary Robison

We

You and I
move to carve out
the faces of the
children we
will never have
on the broad sides of
orange pumpkins—an eye,
a tooth or
two, a nostril, and
the cranium's incision that
in the deranged we call a frontal
lobotomy. In these round fruits
or vegetables we re-insert
light.
The candle flits from
air flowing into this
hand-made nostril, and light
flickers against his chipped enamel
teeth, making it seem to
laugh. I say, "Hey, look, this
one has your crinkling eyes!"
You take my
hand, hold
it to your thigh,
say, "No, don't
play
that way! These are
our gifts
to the masked
children of Hallowe'en who
will litter, like leaves,
our porch, drop wrappers
from gift-candies, then
disappear in-
to the night." Your
thigh, I think, feels
hard like the pumpkin
I held recently
while carving
eyes.

Not Understanding

Why did someone 35 marry someone 78? Why did she die like that all of a sudden? What does his being an artist have to do with anything? Why did his relatives mock him and call him names like "old fool?"

It's hard for me to respond to something I don't understand. The story began so normally and commonly, but the whole thing was just strange to me.

Should their lives be symbolized by pumpkin carving? I think that wouldn't answer all my questions—like why wouldn't she want her own husband to see her wigless and who was calling on the phone?

I wonder if I am dense for not understanding this story? The only thing it makes me think of is that awful gooey smell of pumpkin insides and always thinking I carved the best pumpkin every year. Mine were always evil or distorted because happy ones are boring.

Also, my dad died recently—but not so calmly as the pumpkin lady. If he'd had a wig, it would have been thrown across the room. He was more like the man—a little talent, rarely used, a wasted life.

Harvest

Pumpkins in orange October,
    their sweet, soggy smell
    rising from carved insides
    on wet news—
their fierce pumpkin faces lit by candles—
    glow through the first light of morning,
    the live flame softening their shells
    to mush.
Pumpkins, a child's toy—
    not for May nor December,
    but for late October— usher in
    November and a thanksgiving of sorts,
pumpkins from the brittle vine
    The last sweet
    harvest.

Too Little

To own only a little talent,
to expect too much and like too little,
to see surreal Monets in jack-o-lanterns
whose garish smiles distort in orange flames
is to be awake to possible— and exhausted of— potential.
To see leaves blown in the windswept moon
and only be able to choose literal words
to describe the phenomenon is to lose one's wig
in the night and not notice one's own baldness.
I want to carve pumpkins like the sun
where shadows dance in firelight
and the sweet-hot smell of the removed guts
crackle on the flames and the sky rains
salty green seeds to those literal souls below.
I want a water-color life; to be
drunk with my own living and dying
not to find I was one of those
who only had a spoonful,
    one puny spoonful of talent.

Comment: If we look at the last Re-creation, *Not Understanding,* we find a student who is responding with questions. He has heard the story only once. He doesn't understand. He does not stop the questions. They flow. Yet, with each question, he is really exploring, his mind darting here and there, struggling to understand. But the *Aha!*—the connection comes suddenly in the last paragraph: the leap to his father—the personal connection that illuminates the story and implies his own.

Re-reading these Re-creations after several years in my folder, I am speechless at the capability for such depth, articulateness, empathy, and eloquence in these students, none of whom are English majors, many of whom two decades ago would not have gone to college, and some of whom are second language learners. Michael Polanyi was right:"We know more than we can tell"— particularly analytically or discursively. When we are permitted to give shape to our knowings through a story, we can articulate much of what we have heard, learned, assimilated. Given the chance to become expressive in improvisational fashion, with fear of failure taken out of the equation, these writers show how much they know, how much they can do, feel, think.

Re-Creating Non-Fiction Passages

The next step of experimentation was clear to me: Non-fiction passages, taken out of context. What would students do with parts of essays, parts of textbooks, parts of their professors *hand-outs*? How would they interpret them? How re-create them? Learn from them? Integrate them into their own consciousness? Here are two examples of snippets of someone else's thought, someone else's writing. Not poetry. Not fiction. Parts of essays meant to persuade, to tell, to story that which was important enough to express by one writer or another. The first snippet is from an essay about the importance of poetry:

Poems Are Not Luxuries

Audre Lorde

Poetry is not a luxury. It is a vital necessity of our existence. It forms the quality of the light within which we predicate our hopes and dreams toward survival and change, first made into language, then into idea, then into more tangible action. Poetry is the way we help give name to the nameless so it can be thought. The farthest external horizons of our hopes and fears are cobbled by our poems, carved from the rock experiences of our daily lives.

As they become known and accepted to ourselves, our feelings, and the honest exploration of them, become sanctuaries and fortresses and spawning ground for the most radical and daring of ideas, the house of difference so necessary to change and to the conceptualization of any meaningful action. Right now, I could name at least ten ideas I would once have found intolerable or incomprehensible and frightening, except as they came after dreams and poems. This is not idle fantasy, but the true meaning of "it feels right to me." We can train ourselves to respect our feelings and to discipline (transpose) them into a language that catches those feelings so they can be shared.

Sanctuaries of dreams
are to be found
in the luxurious feeling of poetry.
Carved honesty of
meaningful language
shares more than just words
but horizonless seas of
hope,
fear,
and fantasy.

Giving the Nameless Name
Poetry is necessity
Giving the nameless name
hidden within our hopes and dreams,
trapped within a fortress.
Do not be frightened of
the honest carving in the heart.
Language is a tool
to find true meaning.

What Poetry Is

Poetry is the end product of a necessary process. This process captures in language our feelings, at once carved from the rock of life. The words of our poems help us conceptualize what was previously inconceivable. It gives names to the nameless, turning the unknown into the familiar. We must respect our deepest feelings, those thoughts most likely to escape from our transparent fortress of ideas, lest they be lost forever.

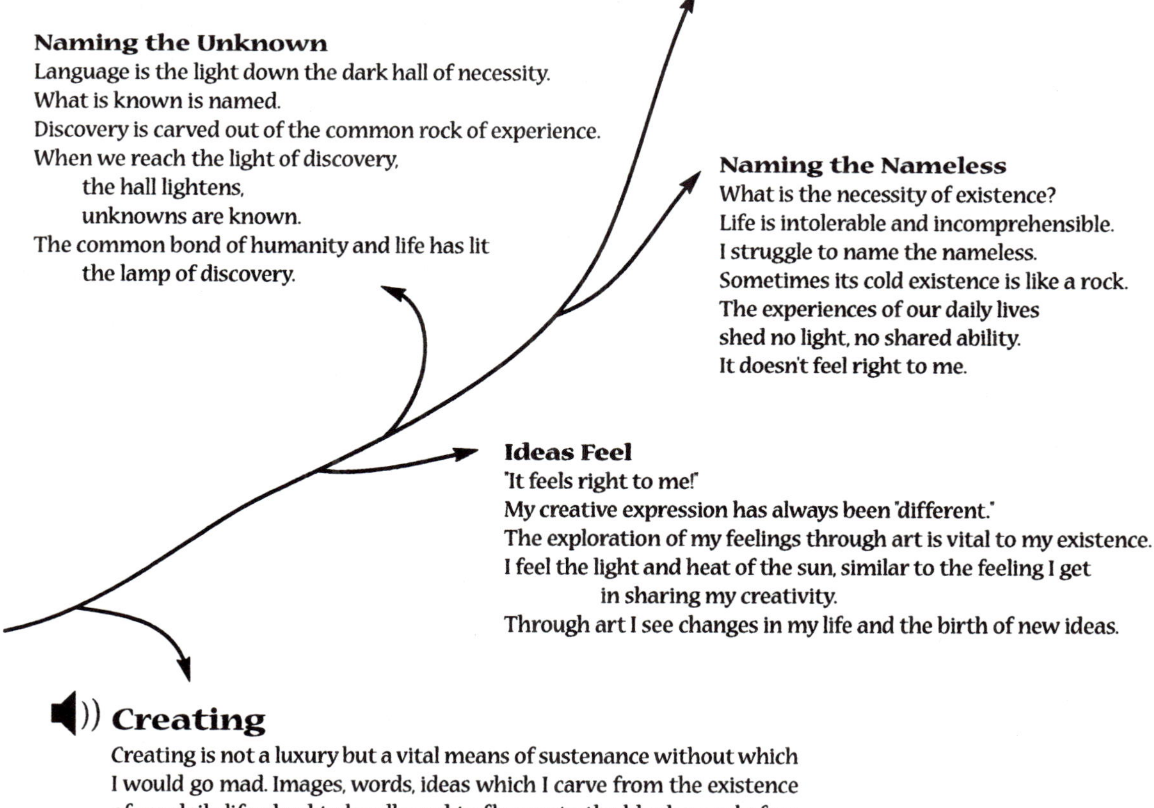

Naming the Unknown

Language is the light down the dark hall of necessity.
What is known is named.
Discovery is carved out of the common rock of experience.
When we reach the light of discovery,
  the hall lightens,
  unknowns are known.
The common bond of humanity and life has lit
  the lamp of discovery.

Naming the Nameless

What is the necessity of existence?
Life is intolerable and incomprehensible.
I struggle to name the nameless.
Sometimes its cold existence is like a rock.
The experiences of our daily lives
shed no light, no shared ability.
It doesn't feel right to me.

Ideas Feel

"It feels right to me!"
My creative expression has always been "different."
The exploration of my feelings through art is vital to my existence.
I feel the light and heat of the sun, similar to the feeling I get
  in sharing my creativity.
Through art I see changes in my life and the birth of new ideas.

Creating

Creating is not a luxury but a vital means of sustenance without which I would go mad. Images, words, ideas which I carve from the existence of my daily life plead to be allowed to flow onto the blank page before me. It frightens me to think of the less beautiful ways I'd vent my anxieties otherwise.

Comment: What more could I have asked of students in an essay exam about the significance of poetry? What more could students have learned from this essay than what they have already exhibited in these three-minute Re-creations? How much more receptive will they be when they are exposed/involved in the reading of a poem because of the way they owned what Audre Lorde wrote by re-creating her ideas in their own words?

I excerpted a second non-fiction passage from famous Spanish poet, Pablo Neruda, which was less of an *idea passage* than a *narrative passage* about the importance to human beings of the intangibles contained in the expressions of any one of the various arts over time and distance:

Childhood and Poetry

Pablo Neruda

One time, in the backyard of our house, I came upon a hole in one of the boards of the fence. I looked through the hole and saw a landscape uncared for, and wild. All of a sudden a hand appeared—a tiny hand of a boy about my own age. By the time I came close again, the hand was gone and it its place there was a marvelous white sheep.

The sheep's wool was faded. Its wheels had escaped. All of this only made it more authentic. I looked back through the hole but the boy had disappeared. I went into the house and brought out a treasure of my own: a pinecone, opened, full of odor and resin, which I adored. I set it down in the same spot and went off with the sheep.

I have been a lucky man. To feel the intimacy of brothers is a marvelous thing in life. To feel the love of people whom we love is a fire that feeds our life, But to feel the affection that comes from those whom we do not know, from those unknown to us, who are watching over our sleep and solitude, over our dangers and our weakenesses—that is something still greater and more beautiful because it widens out the boundaries of our being, and unites all living things.

It won't surprise you then that I attempted to give something resiny, earthlike, and fragrant in exchange. Just as I once left the pinecone by the fence, I have since left my words on the door of so many people who were unknown to me, people in prison, or hunted, or alone.

Transcience

The child whose breath dims the windows
looks out beyond her darkness
to her secret, to outrage not yet learned,
to the fragrance of the past.
Wet fire lingers in
the smell of sorrow
of childhood that ends
too soon after it begins.

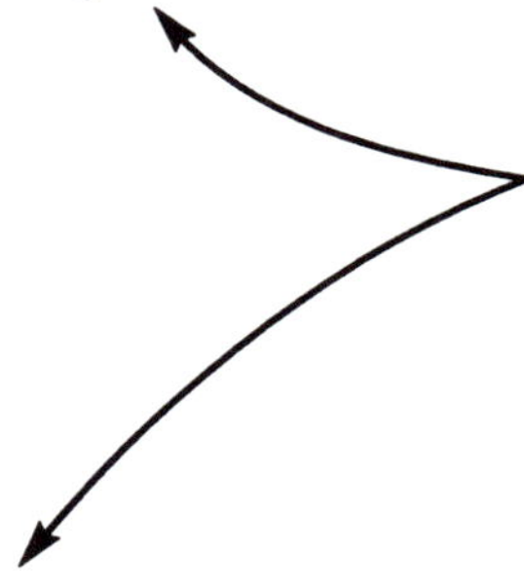

How It Was

As a child I remember feeling old,
that the end of childhood was near,
that my school days would be a remembrance,
a distant fragrance, sorrow, nostalgia
for the teacher who was scared of thunder
for the bus driver who wasn't
for my schoolmates—my twins in yellow slickers, side by side in the school bus.
We were all alike. We were all different.
Where are my comrades from the flotilla?
Where am I? Look on the road map
illuminated by lightning.
The answer is not there.
It lies only in the memory of
steamed bus windows,
shielding me from

Childhood

The windows have become blurred
as my mind yearns to be one with
the ducks as they float along the
pond of my mind's eye.
Today as I drive my own
children to their school rooms
on this rainy, slick day,
I smell the same hint of asphalt I
did on that day long ago.
At that moment I sensed
my childhood's end.
Ah, but for the memories
of a shy little girl yearning to get out—

Memory
In the night rain
in an Oregon ranch house
we foreign sisters listened to the pop
and fizzle of smoke from a broken stone
chewing logs split in the cold,
spoken to in foggy breath and rhythmic tones
while lightning cracked between the rows
of alfalfa that spun out to infinity
from the gravel road to the blue mountains,,
their tops in clouds, black like the smoke
that spiraled above our heads, feeling the room.
And with each crack I squeezed your hand,
the bones small like a small bird, skin freckled,
you squinched your nose and we laughed
to hide the fear of things that cracked
the world open in the dark.
We pulled the ragged blanket over our heads
small bodies drawn closer,
Sisters in the dark,
sisters in the cold,
sisters in the black smoke
and fire and rain and lightning,
over our tired, small home.

School
In the rain we ride the yellow bus
to school, the prison of childhood
where we are separated from nature,
from the wet turbulence outside—
from the turbulence inside as well.
Sitting in rows we stare
at the teacher, overworked and ready
to discipline the one who deviates
from the artificial indoor regimen.
Sitting in rows we stare
through the dim, fogged windows of the room
sniffing the tar-damp smell
of the rain that invites us
    to escape
    and splash in its iridescent puddle,
    and remain childish
    for as long as there is rain.

Smells

I remember the naiveté of childhood, smelling the wet, cut grass creeping in from my open, steamy window. The scent is a trigger, an instant recognition, like the never-forgotten scents of peanut butter and coffee, my mother's pink cold cream.

Peeking outside of seamy windows, I felt safe and confined in my protected world. Outside the rain poured in torrents and lightning flashed across the sky, and I would giggle and point.

I was unaware of the force of the rain, the power of lightning, the terror of forces to come.

The lightning would flash across the sky: spider veins of my mother's legs. One tiny, purple vein, not the body breaking and bending under the burden of life.

The smell comes back, but now I see the storm, not the raindrops trickling down the steamy windows as the smell of grass, freshly cut, creeps in.

Echoes
Finding the intersection of
remembrances
as they ricochet
through our mind.
Signals concurs
the secret places
But the roadmap
is only a façade.

Comment: Prose passages clearly stimulate the same process as do the more compressed poems, therefore making prose passages another vehicle. The Re-creations of Neruda primarily reflect a storm of childhood memories; the focus on *offerings* is minimal. There are only three minutes to write. However, had listeners re-created this prose passage as a way of discovering their own center and to stimulate an idea exchange, the discussion could shift to *offerings* and their significance to Neruda's childhood memory.

T. S. Eliot, *Preludes*

Preludes by T. S. Eliot is a four-part poem totaling fifty-four lines. I wanted to see what kinds of Re-creations would be generated—long, short, divergent, convergent. I wondered what they would do with such a long original in two and a half minutes. I wondered if there would be information overload of such magnitude that the process would be blocked. I also wondered about the content since T.S. Eliot rebelled against the conventionally beautiful or superficially pretty in poetry. Would there be an absence of an emotional attractor?

I here reproduce all thirteen lines of part one and the last seven lines of part four.

Preludes
T. S. Eliot

. . . .
1
. . . .
The winter evening settles down
With smell of steaks in passageways.
Six o'clock.
The burnt-out ends of smoky days.
And now a gusty shower wraps
The grimy scraps
Of withered leaves about your feet
And newspapers from vacant lots;
The showers beat
On broken blinds and chimney-pots,
At the corner of the street
A lonely cab-horse steams and stamps.
And then the lighting of the lamps.

. . . .
4
. . .
I am moved by fancies that are curled
Around these images, and cling:
The notion of some infinitely gentle
Infinitely suffering thing.

Wipe your hand across your mouth, and laugh;
The worlds revolve like ancient women
Gathering fuel in vacant lots.

Façade

I am moved by the images which loom infinite in my winter days of withered leaves— of lonely laughs. As time resumes, I am conscious as the lighting of the lamps reminds me of the morning of visions stretching insistently, gently, like the masquerading of my ancient soul.

Lost

Fearing yourself, you'd rather sleep all day than face the world.
Caught up in what everybody else is doing, you'd rather conform than be free.
Your world is polluted, you search for truth but hide under the sheets when the sun breaks through.
Searching for answers in a material world, you're lost with the rest.

Stretches of Time

The passing of time
does not go unnoticed
for those who observe
the outside, each other.
Rain falls, cleaning a
urine-soaked sidewalk.
You may not be
where you want to be.
The passing of time
does not go unnoticed
for those who observe.

Contrast

The City— a busy, dirty place
Outside, the hustle and bustle
of a mass of people,
faceless, nameless.
Inside, a human being waits alone,
a being
infinitely gentle
and infinitely suffering.

Lack

I hated his gentle hands as he woke me
I hated his strong coffee in the morning
I hated the morning in his frozen apartment
I hated walking home alone on empty streets
I hated his empty eyes as he told me he loved me.

Sordid Life

After the first rain the city's smells only reek louder and damper than before, proudly, for the next rain may wash them away. Damp wool, wet newspapers, urine, oily, dirty street— and yesterday's meatloaf, microwaved, damply escapes from the neighboring apartment when you open the window to smell the wet city cement. Today will be like yesterday. You open a thousand locks on the front door and lock a thousand behind you.

Comment: The re-creators showed no blockage; The constraint of writing for less than three minutes produced relatively short pieces in all cases. The affect-link was very strong; writers without exception picked up on the emotional hook of bleakness, sordidness, sadness, life's ugliness so prevalent in Eliot's images. Although prose Re-creations are generally rare, many were prose, as if the length of Eliot's poem nudged them toward prose. Moreover, the poetic form of T.S. Eliot, despite its length, seems to have steered listeners to be able to express this gloomy vision without sounding sophomoric.

What We Have Learned from This Chapter:

Anything written, including short stories, novels, non-fiction, poetry, memoir, can be compressed beyond anything most of us thought possible. In the past few years a new form, the *short, short*, has appeared and has become very popular. Anything can be re-created: a passage from a novel that unfolds by interaction with their own experience; a paragraph from a textbook which the teacher wants to make sure students understand; a song into a newly-created whole, a painting, transformed into words, not as discourse or analysis, but as a re-contextualized pattern of meaning.

The reason anything can be re-created by almost anyone is captured by poet Elizabeth Bowen's statement: "There's a Me in here, and the me struggles to assert itself, having the deep instinctive urge to live and grow." When we build into our formal curriculum moments of test-free, punishment-free, demand-free learning, the human mind can make exponential growth-leaps, leading to the deep and abiding pleasure of discovery.

CHAPTER NINE

Image into Word, Worlds into Words

> [Around our] sphere whose center may be calculated and whose circumference is physically established, there spin metaphors whose center is everywhere and whose circumference shows itself only through holes in the dark.
>
> — Michael Ayrton

The creative process is untidy, irregular, non-linear in the arts as well as the sciences. Many assume that great scientific discoveries are made logically and by sequential study. Logic and sequence and persistence play an important role, it is true. However, long before we can measure, weigh, articulate, and convince, one's tentative vision, one's emotional attachment to figuring something out can only be glimpsed by indirection and approximation, through fuzzy images that serve as signals to mental/emotional exploration. I can think of no better illustration than this true story of Einstein's attempt to describe relativity theory.

Much of what we learn is learned intuitively and by indirection and a Re-creation is first and foremost an expression of indirection. It is not frontal assault; it is not analysis; it is not knowing beforehand what we are going to say, make, or do. Rather, it is exploratory, often meandering. As we saw in Chapter Seven, great painters have always learned by experimenting with, playing with, synthesizing, expanding on, or reinterpreting, the paintings of those who have gone before, just as Shakespeare reinterpreted Holinshed. But artists have also struggled to cross over from one domain to another, re-creating a painting in words, as Ferlinghetti does below, drawing on a painting of Gustav Klimt, or transforming words into music, as Schubert did with over 600 art songs. They have metamorphed poems into paintings, as Charles Demuth did with a William Carlos Williams poem. Other artists have taken their inspiration from a dra-

Theory of Relativity
(as recalled by Dr. Paul Witty)

Professor Einstein went to a party one night and the hostess said, "Professor Einstein will tell us the meaning of relativity."

"I shall tell you a story instead," he said:

I was going down the street the other day with a blind friend and I remarked that I should like a glass of milk.

"What is milk?" asked my blind friend.
"A white liquid," I answered.
"Liquid I know, but what is white?"
"The color of swan's feather."
"Feathers I know, but what is a swan?"
"A bird with a crooked neck."
"Neck I know, but what is crooked?"
By that time I had grown impatient
and I seized his arm and bent it.
I said,"This is crooked."
Then I straightened his arm and said,
"This is straight."
Ah," said my blind friend,
"now I know what you mean by milk."

Then Mr. Einstein turned to his hostess and said, "Would you like me to tell you more about relativity?"

matic plays and have turned it into a ballet, sculptures, or music inspired by fairy stories, and all combinations in-between. It is a primal human hunger to re-create something in one's own medium, perhaps to understand it better, perhaps to get at its essence, perhaps to learn why the attraction is so strong, perhaps, as Delacroix pointed out, to complete the incompleteness that artists feel in a work that preceded them or to answer a question that arose from the work.

From Image to Word:

Metaphorming a visual image—an already created artifact—into a Re-creation is no more a copy than the Re-creation of a poem. Asked to look at a visual whole—a painting, sculpture, photograph, knowing we will DO something with it, in wer search for meaning, we are nudged into an emotional response to the whole—perhaps first only of like or dislike, of Yes or No. Then, as we cluster what we think we are seeing, itself a metaphorming process of image into word, we gather observations that—gradually or suddenly—illuminate our own emerging patterns of meaning as we scan. It may not be earth-shattering; it may not even be much. But, as we cluster what we see, we notice more and more, both what is actually out there and the pattern that is taking shape within. When the actual writing begins, we improvise rapidly, transforming the images our brain is struggling to make meaning with into words; the rapid improvisation is too fast, too immediate to generate anything but approximation, hunches, guesses that fit our internal world map. In the welter of thought and feeling, our minds tends to make unplanned metaphoric leaps. And because of the nonlinearity of the process itself, our minds are surprised into a pattern of meaning.

How Do Works of Visual Art Inspire Us?

An art image expresses something, just as a poem does, or music, or dance. We may not know what or how, but the whole of it makes an impact by evoking a feeling in anyone willing to go beyond merely looking to seeing. When we cluster a painting around a blank center, our wide attention gradually reaches beyond any narrow focus to name any tentative insight in the blank center. This naming allows us to begin the metaphorming process into words on a page. The work of art, filtered through our experiential sieves, has an emotional meaning which is simultaneously beyond it and beyond us. The significance is not in the painting alone, nor is it in us alone, but it is the synergy between us and it, between the meaning-pattern already created by the artist and the meaning-patterns evolving in us. This metaphorming process is facilitated by the existing image complex of the painting. By metaphorming the painting in words, we have created our own expressive form so that it is readable, interpretable, tangible on a page.

Everything in life is a Re-creation, a variation, a spin-off. Words are often re-created into music, music into paintings, paintings into dances, not to mention musical metaphorms, like Bach's and Mozart's, all variations on a theme.

Picasso, according to many art historians, is the prime example of an ensemble artist in the twentieth century who not only borrowed relentlessly but who, in doing so, used most things he borrowed to express them in a new way to reflect his own expanding world map. What he borrowed was not the thing itself but the INFORMATION he got from his borrowing from past artists, past cultures, past techniques. He was not interested in copying; he was interested in

learning. In short, he was jump-starting his creative impulses.

British sculptor Michael Ayrton wrote that Picasso's genius lay in his ability to transform his discoveries and showed that Picasso had stated his creative intentions in his answer to his own rhetorical question: "What fundamentally is a painter?" His answer was: "He's a collector who wishes to obtain a collection by making himself the paintings he likes. It's like that and then it becomes something else." This epigrammatic manifesto illustrates Picasso's consciousness in deliberately building on others' already existing patterns of meaning as a vehicle for discovering his own.

So it is with Re-creations. Living artifacts stimulate the imagination of others, continuing to evolve in other minds as long as there are people interacting with it, learning from it, reinterpreting it. Shakespeare stays great because each age interprets his plays from a different angle. In a sense, Shakespeare, as each age interacts with his Re-creations, keeps developing as they are recontextualized into our lives. In one sense Holinshed lives because Shakespeare re-created the *Chronicles* in a way that was expressive of his imagination, his time, the Renaissance. Shakespeare continues to live because 500 years later his plays are still living artifacts which human beings are driven to interpret again and again. Shakespeare's plays continue to be performed on stages from new angles, are re-made into movies, are adapted, borrowed from, synthesized to our ends, after almost 500 years. (Look at the recent successes of *Shakespeare in Love, Romeo and Juliet, Hamlet.*)

Image into Word

I began to experiment with visual images, always surprised by the results. It did not matter whether images were realistic or abstract or in-between. Here is one student's brief Re-creation of a Mondrian painting, along with her inverse cluster and her named center:

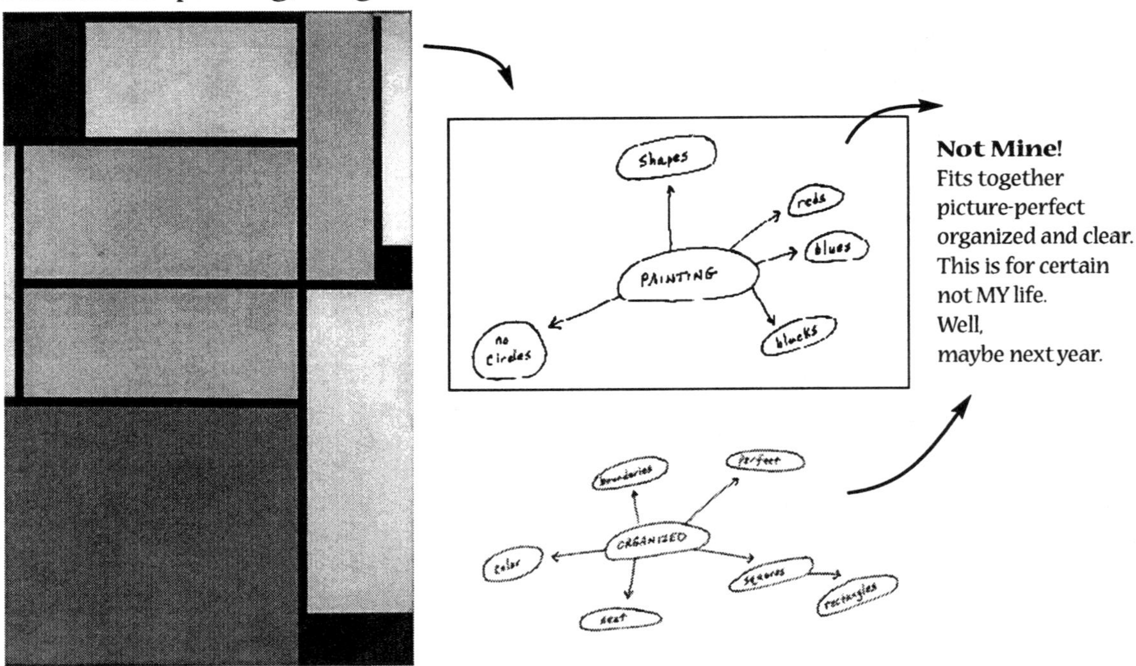

How readily we metaphorm an already-existing visual artifact of someone else's making to jump-start our own creative impulses. I experimented further with an image which has haunted me for years, this by modern Russian painter, Pavel Tchelitschev. His work elicited a stunning variety of Re-creations

Tchelitchev

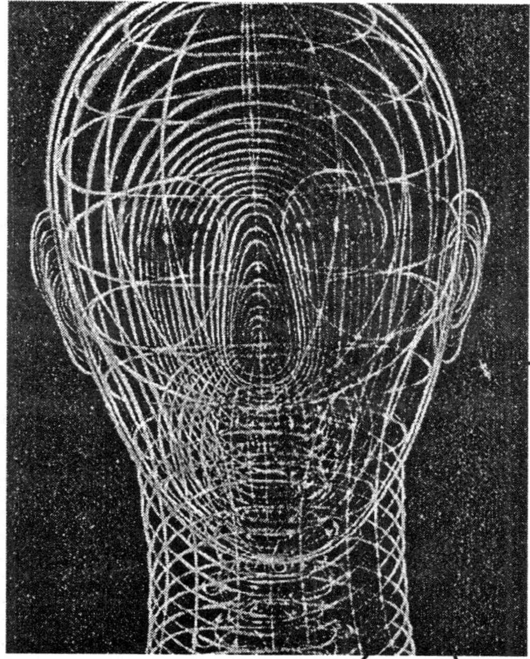

Please Hear Me

Can you hear me?
I am speaking—
not out loud.
If I spoke out loud, I would scream.
Nothing but screams,
screams of joy,
screams of hatred,
screams of passion
screams of pain.
Can you hear me?

Cycling

The challenge of thought,
thoughts that don't connect,
thoughts that just see objects.
The challenge: Can you accept it?
Can you see it?
Can you hear the thoughts
circling, cycling
meaninglessly?

Nothing

The shape of nothing,
the space of nothing,
Nothing, in shape,
nothing in the center.
The formless forming lines of thought,
the bright yellow lines
circling but . . . not
forming but. . . not.
It is the thought,
the bright, yellow line,
the bright line of thought—
the fingerprint of our soul.

Tchelitchev's Face

I wonder about vision:
Is it transparent?
Does it have limits?
What is its nature?
If I see, am I seen
If I know, am I known?
I am unfathomable.
I am open. I am closed.
I am mute.

Eternal Emergence

The journey without destinations
as vital as threats
of the heart

I listen for sound vibrations
for the song of all beings
touched by light waves,
all who go through transformation
who move through the cocoon,
the vortex of change.

These are my family—
as visible as the shroud of Turin—
who travel by the topographic map:
the mirror of the spirit.

Bullet Line

I promise to think like a bullet. I promise
to spin as the riflings of the barrel spin.
I will not look to left or right,
marrying this path and no other.
Please give me up; let me move
as does a precise argument
from the axiom of the firing pin
to the theorem of a creature's conclusion.

Who else can hope to dream
a dream of a single dimension?

Please let me alone. Go listen
to falling water— if you have ears.

Circles of thought

Is there a reason?
Does life always fit in,
balanced solidly between
what is and what could be.
Circles of thought intertwined,
each one a reflection of the other,
the same, yet inverted.
Perfection is found in the symmetrical
truthful organic form,
found in the veins of the plants
that breathe
and in our minds that think.

On Not Opening

My innermost feelings are usually
buried deep inside.
I fear that if I share myself,
I will be naked, alone.
The vibrations that seek their way
out of this cavern I call my soul
sometimes force me into seclusion.
I share myself with only a chosen few.

Life Lines

The lines on a face are the contour map of her life. The curving, branding creases illuminate every road she's traveled. They form a record of experiences, spiraling out from the center of her being. Follow the lines at the corners of her eyes and mouth. They crinkle in celebration of the love and laughter that she is.

Comment: People have an almost visceral reaction to this work. This visceral reaction often leads to Re-creations which emphasize the affect-link as well as the story link discussed in Chapters Three and Five. Often, after re-creating, the Re-creators were surprised at the many different *centers* that were discovered, how they were rarely identical, how often they reflected similar responses, how the titles changed the initial center. The first was BULLET, turning into *Bullet Line.* The second was FACE; the third, EMERGENCE. Others ranged from NOT OPENING and NOTHINGNESS to the poignant *PLEASE HEAR ME.*

Metaphorming a Metaphorm:

I wondered what students would do if I went one step further by showing an painting projected on a wall while at the same time reading a poem inspired by of a painting by Gustav Klimt into a poem. I knew the stimulus would be double: that is, they would be simultaneously guided by the image as well as the poem filtered through their unique experiential sieve, then being enfolded into their own expanding world map.

Given the double stimulus of image and poem, my students re-created the following metaphorms:

Klimt, **The Kiss**

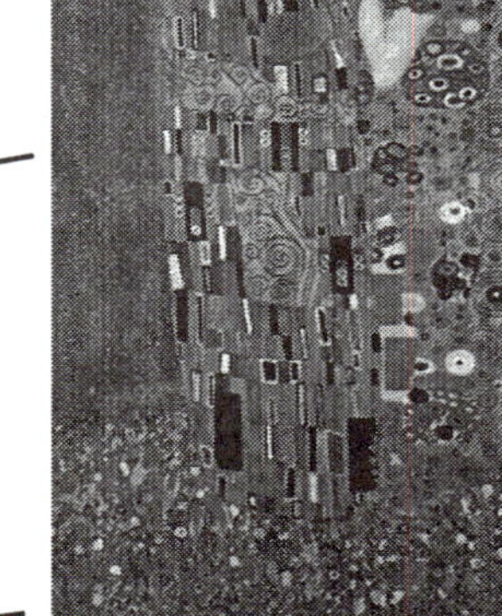

Romance?

He spies her from across the dirty room,
a beer belch from the massive jello belly
passes through his snotty lip hair
and engulfs a fly whirling dead.
The jeans jostle as the jock jumps forward,
the tobacco smoke trailing like a flume
in back of the world's sloppiest behind.
She turns a tricky step,
and he flies past, winding up
outside by his big wheels on big track.
Once there, he grabs his stick,
lays some rubber, and is gone,
the STP sticker and macho killer dog in the back
but a memory.

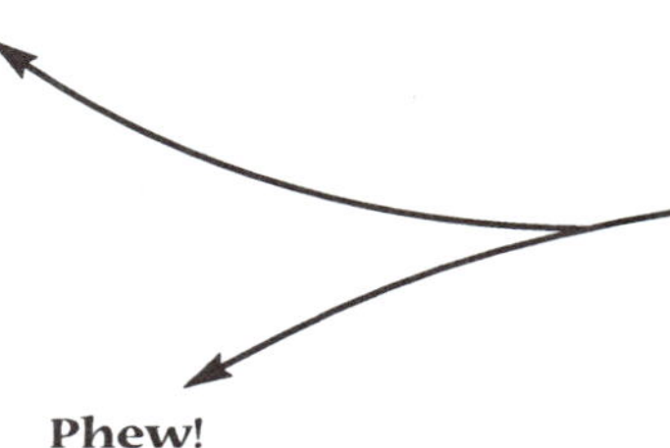

Phew!

As he turned his face to her,
she thought, "Oh, he must had
a lot of garlic for dinner
last night!" End…

He

The blue stars surround them,
their embrace is hungry,
controlled by her stiff arms.
His passionate insistence
cannot unfold
the petal of her love
enveloped by her tight breasts
and tangerine lips.
He pulls her toward him
only to be rebuffed
with the side of her cheek,
the forearms against him,
as if to say:
"Not here, in this field of flowers,
will we be one."

Closed Eyes

The grip made her kneel
on the flowery bed.
The urgency of his fingers
caught her neck and held her
at the right length.
He could not see her pressed breasts,
her tense feet,
her hand shaped like a claw.
He could only see her closed
eyes and tangerine lips

Force Doesn't Work

Neither stifled passion nor force
can bend upwards the dead swan neck.
She kneels tense, silent, still,
as urgent hunger crimps
the neck with bare, stiff, plywood hands.
Hinged knuckles try to make her turn,
try to pry the quilted eyes and pursed lips.
Glass and damp nakedness commingle—
uncomfortable stance, the bending unmanaged,
burnt desire burns out.
She remains closed.

SHORT STORY ON A PAINTING OF GUSTAV KLIMT

Lawrence Ferlinghetti

They are kneeling upright on a flowered bed
He
has just caught her there
and holds her still
Her gown
has slipped down
off her shoulder
He has an urgent hunger
His dark head
bends to hers
hungrily
And the woman the woman
turns her tangerine lips from his
one hand like the head of a dead swan
draped down over
his heavy neck
the fingers
strangely crimped
tightly together
her other arm doubled up
against her tight breast
her hand a languid claw
clutching his hand
which would turn her mouth
to his
her long dress made
of multicolored blossoms
quilted on gold
her Titian hair
with blue stars in it
And his gold
harlequin robe
checkered with
dark squares
Gold garlands
stream down over
her bare calves &
tensed feet
Nearby there must be
a jeweled tree
with glass leaves aglitter
in the gold air
It must be
morning
in a faraway place somewhere
They
are silent together
as in a flowered field
upon the summer couch
which must be hers
And he holds her still
so passionately
holds her head to his
so gently so insistently
to make her turn
her lips to his
Her eyes are closed
like folded petals
She will not open
He is not
the One

Devoid

Gold jewels,
tense, silent,
clutching, captive.
Is it love?
Tangerine lips
glittering trees,
summer's couch.
Hunger, lust;
Clasping, clawing.
Devoid of love.
Dead swan.

Who over Whom?

SHE is draped over HIM
like a towel robe—the
kind you get forever at Holiday Inns.
Her long claws peel at his heart:
"Don't you like me?
You said you loved me?"
"Yeah, he says but that was last night.
Today is a new morning
and you ain't no garland flower.

Sealed

Eyes closed,
I can pretend that you are he
that you are the one I love.
If I do not open,
I will not be dirtied by the wetness.
With lips sealed, I am still my own.

Frozen

He pulls my head to his
with such urgency, I pull away.
What once was a flowered bed
is now a brown and frozen meadow,
clutching to the memory of what was.
I hold on,
but I know
he is not the one.

Comment: The affect-line, because of the double stimulus, is often radical because Klimt's painting has almost become a visual cliché of *love*, reproduced on greeting cards and posters. In listening to Ferlinghetti's interpretation, they are usually shocked because they have rarely moved beyond the beautiful image, the lovers, the romantic stance of the couple. Suddenly, having written, they scan the painting once more, for the first time seeing hints in the painting of nuances they hadn't seen before, becoming aware of the distinction between the expected and the expressed, between what they wanted to see and what must be seen, between nuance and bald statement.

Reversing the Metaphorms:

Often I reverse the process, asking students to re-create only the painting before they hear a poet's Re-creation of a painting. Only afterward do we listen to the poem, eliciting totally different meanings, particularly in terms of positive or negative affect-links, positive or negative story-links. Without the Ferlinghetti metaphorm many Re-creations are unabashedly idealized.

Students identified in strongly emotional ways with Edvard Munch's *The Scream*.

Going
Alone and wandering wordlessly
he tries to connect by getting out
but he can't
connect.
He can't even see, he can't
understand the horror; the icy
water feels so good as it
rises, rises, rises to his
knees, hip
torso, lip.
his silent scream,
frozen hard,
sinks into eternal numbness.

End
Guilty, they require fire
to expunge sterile spirits.
She runs to the bridge
and creates her own salvation
on the rocks below.

On the Page
When my soul screams for release,
and the lines of my eyes drip blood
and sweat and tears fall in the shape
of words, black words, on my page;
when this happens I feel squeezed
through a press of possibility
that wrings the life in liquid ink
condensed, potent, distancing.
Like a hunk of garlic in a press,
I shove myself through the spaces
and redefine the matter I am left with.
Bake me. Eat me. Breathe me.
I am here.

Edvard Munch, **The Scream**

Screaming
The scream
high-pitched and deafening,
head in her hands,
eyes open wide,
mouth hung open in terror,
the sound penetrating
the still air.
No one listens.
No one helps.
Alone in darkness,
night folding in on her,
she screams
all alone.

Choosing
Sometimes, when life catches up with us our initial reaction is fear or confusion. When the grain goes against us, we feel a sense of panic or momentary loss. The world can seem dark or devoid of light. But life demands more than panic. It demands we overcome and get beyond. The crossing of the chasm may be hard, but we have others to turn to and feel support. We can, if we choose, convert the darkness into energy to overcome. Only we can discern what constitutes the light we need to move forward. That is our choice.

Re-creations are a way of catching affect-links for later expansion of an improvisation. For example, this student wrote the first piece on the spot. Later he chose to expand—and revise—this Re-creation into an essay because he was surprised and delighted by his initial Re-creation.

Hokusai, **The Great Wave**

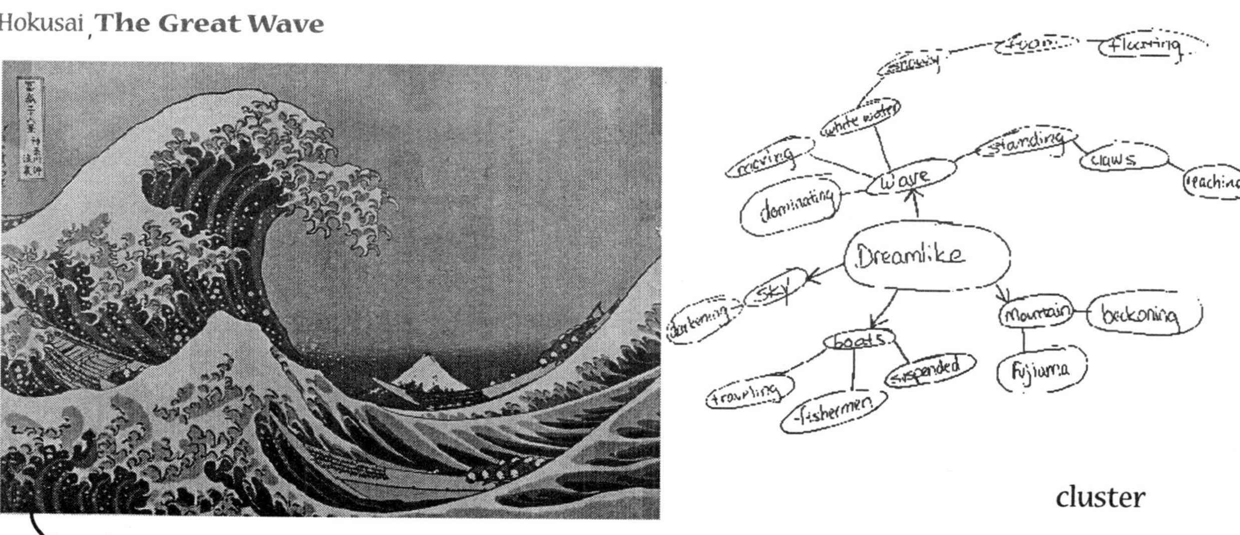

Hokusai

Clustering what I see in Hokusai's painting shows me three dramatic and related things: the overwhelming wave, the tiny men in the little boat, and the steady silent mountain. I'm not sure how they go together, but I'm certain there is a relationship. What is the painter trying to tell us about life? That water destroys? That mountains endure? That human beings are vulnerable? I'm not sure. I only know that this painting speaks to me about something, something important, I need to learn.

The mystery of Hokusai and of his emotional response impelled this writer to explore further that nuanced *something important* he needed to learn. Ultimately, this second draft became a formal essay. So here we have a painting, filtered through the experiential sieve of this writer, yielding a three minute response. It will not leave him alone, so he sets out to write more about the mystery he doesn't yet understand. Psychiatrist and futurist Charles Johnston said that "expression is not an appendix to knowing but the process by which something becomes knowing." We can see here the first two stages which lead to greater understanding because this writer expressed it.

Hokusai,'s Dream, Our Fear

To examine Hokusai's *The Great Wave*, and really suspend yourself in it, is to put yourself in a dream-like state. It contains many of the paradoxical qualities found in a dream.

The whole painting is unreal, yet more real than reality itself. The wave, boats, and men seem to be moving, but at the same time standing still. The sky gets darker as it gets closer to the horizon with Mount Fujiama in the distance, as if to beckon the dreamer.

The waves and ocean are topped by whitewater which seems to float, as if detached from the water. The wave seems to be a collection of many claws, reaching to grab the fishermen, yet never quite reaching them.

All of these things happening: the wave reaching, the men rowing, Mount Fuji beckoning, seem to work cooperatively in the unfolding of a great destiny. The destiny itself is a paradox: The fishermen following their own will, yet blindly following fate and the forces of nature; the ocean and wave, a force which is spontaneous, yet all within the ordered will of God; the mountain, a sign of steadiness amid turmoil, yet too passing away.

Dreams are our own code of life-symbols. When we awaken, we see these same symbols in the real world. Do we really know the difference between dream and reality?

What we have learned from this chapter:

In the translation of images into words, the eye, scanning the whole, connects us to the affect-link, in turn, connects us to story, to discovery, to growth. Learning is a primary characteristic of the human. Learning depends on both continuity and change. Learning is is a mixing of the novel; and the known, to bring the unknown in line with the familiar and the previous learning in line with the challenge of the new.

Reflection is also a way of learning. One way to reflect is to attend to something already created; and, instead of being merely an observer, to re-create it for ourselves here, now, in this moment. A second way is to reflect on what we have made to see how it is different from the first and what we have learned from it, what we discovered, what we wonder about, what surprised us, what we learned, are learning, will learn when we attend differently. This process of opening emotionally and intellectually is triggered by the re-creative process.

CHAPTER TEN

Multilogue

INTERLINKING MINDS

> We humanize what is going on in the world and in ourselves only by speaking of it, and in the course of speaking of it we learn to be human.
> —Hannah Arendt

Multilogue is not just communication between but among several—or among many. Multilogue interlinks minds in special ways. It is a conscious, deliberate way of entering into others' minds, other angles, other ways of seeing in order to leap into moments of surprise. It is a reaching beyond into the extension of self into empathy. It is the opening of one's boundaries into creative and emotional expansion instead of contraction. Multilogue makes us aware that, to any conversation, we bring our many knowings which we have gleaned from many sources. Multilogue is combinatory, exploratory, flexible, fuzzy, diverse, expressive. At the macro level, multilogue is deep awareness of our interconnectedness as human beings in a global network of minds.

Multilogue is a welter of voices thrown together, echoing outward— the opposite of separating out. Multilogue is the opposite of single-mindedness, which all too often results in the belief that learning must mostly be like heaving bricks, or that tortured analysis is the only way to enter a text, as this writer makes clear:

Introduction to Poetry
Billy Collins

I ask them to take a poem
and hold it up to the light
like a color slide

or press an ear against its hive.

I say drop a mouse into a poem
and watch it probe its way out,

or walk inside a poem's room
and feel the walls for a light switch.

I want them to waterski
across the surface of a poem
waving at the author's name on the shore.

But all they want to do
is tie the poem to a chair with rope
and torture a confession out of it.

They begin beating it with a hose
to find out what it really means.

We have grown to believe that learning is dissecting, ripping apart, analyzing, in large part because that is we have learned learning is, what we thought we had to do, what our students think they are supposed to do. And, indeed they do. They must address the parts, the nitty gritties, but there are other, powerful characteristics of learning, the sense of the whole as it speaks to us without full knowledge of the particulars. Re-creation does nothing more than remind us of our skill at taking in the whole, even when we don't know much about the specifics. Re-creation is a concrete mold-breaking strategy, an experimentation with expressive forms. We need new processes and forms through multiple kinds of writing. The use of poetic forms to break through to surprise, to improvisation, to the roots of the formal approaches to learning, grows out of such rootedness.

This final chapter gives examples of the deeply collaborative nature of creativity: How we do not accomplish it alone as if we were in a vacuum. How we can accomplish it by re-creating from one medium to another. How creativity, allowed to iterate, is infinite in its manifestations. How, in the most effective learning, we both transcend AND incorporate.

A poem heard—and listened to— revises the fledgling writer just as much as the fledgling writer impacts the poem. Fledgling writers, by a process of ce-creation, are asked to do the unthinkable: to respond in two or three minutes to something in they heave heard once, then twice, then write—jogging them into surprise, just as the poets are, about what emerged for them. Instead of being an OBJECT of scrutiny, the poem itself becomes a participatory learning act—and in most cases, a creative act. The creative act is learning at its most memorable, its most intense, its most revealing, its most fruitful, and its longest-lasting.

We can generate these leaps in learning, even with the most mundane of content, the most dutiful of reading tasks. Take, for example, a science essay in a general education class. Take a passage from that essay, ask them to listen, then ask them to DO something with it. The cognitive leap from PASSIVE learning to ACTIVE learning is almost always made via surprise. That affect link of surprise becomes the emotional bridge between the thing to be learned and the actual learning of it.

> It is difficult to stand forth in one's growing if one is not permitted to live through the states of one's unripeness, clumsiness, unreadiness, as well as one's grace and aptitude.
>
> —M.C. Richards

Why the Sound of Words instead of the Print of Words —Why a CD?

> The deepening need for words to express our thoughts and feelings which, we are sure, are all the truth that we shall ever experience... makes us listen to words when we hear them, loving them and feeling them, makes us search the sound of them ...
>
> —Wallace Stevens, *The Necessary Angel*

In an age of print, poems are primarily read in books, text is read in textbooks. Today, given the technological impact of the aural and iconic revolutions, sound and image have great impact on expanding minds. Words are heard again in startling new ways. Some straws in the wind, apart from the multi-media technologies are the *poetry slams* which are springing up around the country, such as at Mark Smith's *Green Mill* in Chicago, at which poets and wannabe poets congregate to HEAR poems recited or read so they can listen, really listen, to the magic of the word (A straw in the wind of the iconic revolution can be observed in each week's *Journal of the American Medical Association* which features a painting, discussed with great sensitivity inside the journal itself).

Progressive Re-creations of Re-creations: An Iterative Phenomenon

As we've seen, Re-creations generate a concrete awareness of how the creative process *feels.* In encouraging, inviting learners to become creators themselves, they become aware that creating is what human minds do—as well as memorizing or analyzing or interpreting.

In addition to experiencing the pleasure that accompanies creating something on a page, we become aware of how our creative thoughts interact with one another. When our thoughts and images interlink with those of others, our thinking expands. Patterns emerge as our minds connect with one another. As they connect, we open to potential, growth, and change. Our range increases. We make learning leaps. We participate in creative the forms of expression. When we do, we discover new meanings—and we are changed by them. In changing we expand our vistas, become more receptive, mentally more flexible.

When we re-create, we are nudged beyond our present understanding of ourselves, of what we *know* to this point, and of the context of our world, into something unfamiliar, somethng previously ungraspable. This is the meeting-place of minds. In the moment of transfer of meaning, something silent and invisible happens. Relationship. Relating to our predecessors, our multiple cultural environments, each other, each others' minds. The interacting multiplicities of experience assure that each Re-creation will look different from every other. Minds interacting, minds changing, and minds sharing also interlink learning styles, taking multiple pathways of multiple registers in multiple tones. Yet, the amazing thing is that all echo recursive human themes.

Almost by accident, I discovered that Multilogue is dramatically magnified when we engage in Re-creations of Re-creations in which each individual mind gives off an expanded form each time a new voice tackles it, no matter how naive or skilled that voice.

A Re-creation of a Re-creation is reminiscent of a play within play, as we've seen in Shakespeare's *Hamlet*, of a painting within a painting, of delicately nested Chinese boxes, of the passing of the baton of relay runners who, together, learn to excele and to use their individual

strengths to cooperate in excelling.

Sculptor Michael Ayrton makes the point that, "as the diffusion continues, the germinal image spreads outwards by means of a series of adaptations and derivations," the way of most great inventions which are developed and transformed over time. Thus, Re-creations illustrate the human mind's capacity to EXPAND and INCORPORATE, EXPAND AND INCORPORATE, in a potentially never-ending feedback loop. This natural mental process leads to ever-evolving tangible creative acts, involving an ever-widening circle of learners in creative acts.

Let me give several specific examples of Re-creations of Re-creations. We have already seen the following poem by Donald Justice in an earlier chapter which Maurya Simon re-created (perhaps somewhat self-consciously) in her poem, *Women at 30* (p. 87).

Example one of progressive Re-creations:

Men at Forty

Donald Justice

Men at forty
Learn to close softly
The doors to rooms they will not be
Coming back to.

At rest on a stair landing,
They feel it
Moving beneath them now like the deck of a ship,
Though the swell is gentle.

And deep in mirrors
They rediscover
The face of the boy as he practices tying
His father's tie there in secret

And the face of that father,
Still warm with the mystery of lather.
They are more fathers than sons themselves now.
Something is filling them, something

That is like the twilight sound
Of the crickets, immense,
Filling the woods at the foot of the slope
Behind their mortgaged houses.

Here is Robin's 3 minute Re-creation of *Men at Forty*

No Return

I won't be coming back
to these rooms
I close each year.
Darkness fills them,
spilling out from under the doors.

The hallway has only
so many doors as it is,
and I fear each turn toward
the light from a window
and my hand slipping off
the last brass knob.

And here is Kate's Re-creation—she has not heard the original Justice poem— of Robin's Re-creation above :

What I Fear

I fear the light glaring off brass door knobs
urging me to enter
rooms,
rooms spilling darkness,
and ghostly hallways
that dare me to turn,
always turn.
And in the turn from light to dark,
dark to light,
my hand on the knob
leads me toward the unknown.

Example two of progressive Re-creations is based on Anne's Re-creation of Denise Levertov's poem, *Writing in the Dark* (p. 20):

Idea
These shapes I have made
are almost letters.
I can almost read them. And now,
I am sure there was a vision there
that was so clear, so pure
that its urgency was like the blooming
of a flower, the flight of a bird.
Now the sun has risen with its own
urgency,
and I can see now that there must have been
something more,
but I cannot remember exactly
what it was.
— Anne

And here follows Robin's Re-creation of the Anne's Re-creation—Robin not having seen or heard the Levertov original:

Recital
The dream dissolved
like the flight of a bird into
the treeline.
I was sure it was a vision
and that any moment
God would whisper His name
so that only I could hear,
and I would recite it urgently
like the sunlight recites
the shapes all around me.
—Robin

Example three of progressive Re-creations from Sylvia's Re-creation (below) of Nan Fry's *The Plum* (p. 22)

Food
It is not merely sustenance,
not merely the fuel that lights our energy.
Eating, when done well
(though not necessarily well-done)
is an orgy for the senses:
Colors explode and meld on a delicate plate
as ecstatic odors assail the nose,
encouraging the tongue to quiver,
salty saliva to flow.
Then, broken down and blended,
the delightful mush
slides delectably down the silken throat,
leaving room for more.
—Sylvia

Sylvia's Re-creation served as the basis for Robin's Re-creation, neither one of them having seen or heard the original:

Fuel
Finish your vegetables.
Don't play with your food.
Just eat what's put in front of you.
Children in China would love to have this.
Leave room for more.
—Robin

A fourth set of examples of progression is John's Re-creation of Al Young's *Chemistry* (p. 49)

Moon
The moon is legendary,
connecting me to the universe,
to life.
The moon connects me
to the dark side
of the night—to blood.
The moon connects me to the elements:
water, hydrogen, nitron.
Chemistry.
The moon is legendary,
connecting me to the dark side,
fear and the light side, joy,
swimming into freedom,
turning away from the
chains of the dark.

And here is Robin's Re-creation of John's, Robin not having seen or heard the original poem:

Bridge
The dark side of night
connects me to the moon,
chained,
whose legendary face
nevertheless
turns toward me
from the universe.

A fifth set of progressions is based on Jim's Re-creation of John Ciardi's *Sometimes Running* (p. 42)

Clockwork
There was once a man who prided himself on time conservation, who got enough sleep each night, who ate at a certain time and was never late from lunch, who did work on weekends if need be, and never, never, ever, let go. I wonder if he ever tasted what he ate, rolled his food over and over and over on his tongue.

—Jim

Robin's Recreation of Jim's Recreation:

No Time
There once was a man
who had no time.
He ate the clock
over and over and over
and he never, ever, ever
wondered about anything.
—Robin

And Kate's Re-creation of Robin's Re-creation

Circling
Over & over & over
the clock hands circle
over & over & over.
There is no time
there is no
time.
—Kate

The sixth set of examples is based on Matt's Re-creation of Gwendolyn Brooks' *Hunchback Girl, She Thinks of Heaven* p. 44). (Amazingly, Matt seems to have made a leap to Picasso's *Man with a Guitar*—or perhaps to Wallace Stevens' *Man with the Blue Guitar*—which may well be visual to verbal Re-creations in their own right—here integrated by a student: in a piece that speaks of his father):

Man Playing a Blue Guitar
My father,
blue man playing a guitar,
Picasso's Blue Man on a wall, in paint
outlined by straight lines,
confined, framed—
inside, lines of vision freely roaming
around the colored strokes, aimlessly.
I can hear him plucking a song,
following the notes to wherever they lead him,
a bricoleur on a stringed box,
plucking, plucking, plucking,
following the Muse—
just playing.
—Matt

Below is Robin's Re-creation of Matt's:

Paradox
Following the notes
on a wall, in paint,
the blue man
with his guitar made
all of angles,
must stop the song
when he comes to a window.

The the seventh set of examples of progression is based on Merritt's Re-creation of Wallace Stevens famous *Thirteen Ways of Looking at a Blackbird*.

Variation on a Theme
Black bird.
Black bird.
Waiting, waiting,
his eye rotating
moving over
20 snowy mountains,
his eye a reflection
of innuendos
as a river moving
frozen icicles forming
a glass coach, a
glass shadow of
rhythm that
carried a thin man
and sad woman
out of sight at
the edge of the
3 minds as they
moved into one:
the man and the
woman and, yes
the black bird
together in the
green light on
the cedar limbs.
Winds of fear
whirling, whirled,
erase the inflection,
the mood, the meaning.
—Merritt

Robin's Recreation of Merritt's Re-creation follows:

Pulling Winter Behind
As a river moving —
as a thin man driving a
sad woman
over twenty snowy mountains
in a glass coach —
the blackbird pulls winter behind him
on wheels of ice that begin to sing.
What can he do
but keep going?

The eighth set of examples of progression is Re-creation of Marjorie Maddox's *Elocution Lessons* (p. 56):

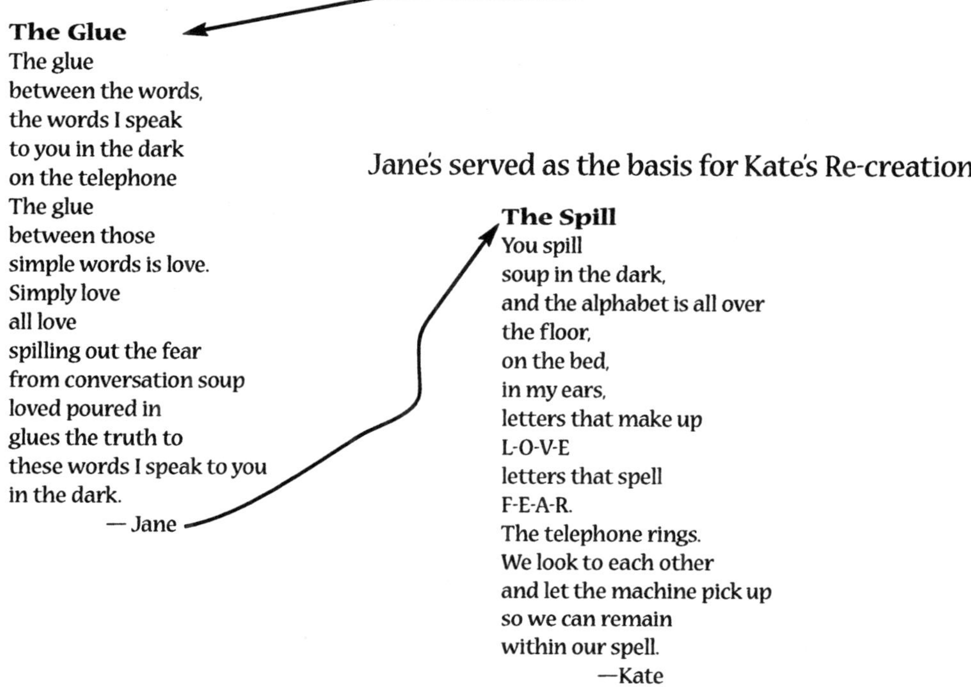

The Glue
The glue
between the words,
the words I speak
to you in the dark
on the telephone
The glue
between those
simple words is love.
Simply love
all love
spilling out the fear
from conversation soup
loved poured in
glues the truth to
these words I speak to you
in the dark.
— Jane

Jane's served as the basis for Kate's Re-creation

The Spill
You spill
soup in the dark,
and the alphabet is all over
the floor,
on the bed,
in my ears,
letters that make up
L-O-V-E
letters that spell
F-E-A-R.
The telephone rings.
We look to each other
and let the machine pick up
so we can remain
within our spell.
—Kate

The ninth set of progressions is Kate's Re-creation of Philip Dacey,s *Proofreading* (p.94):

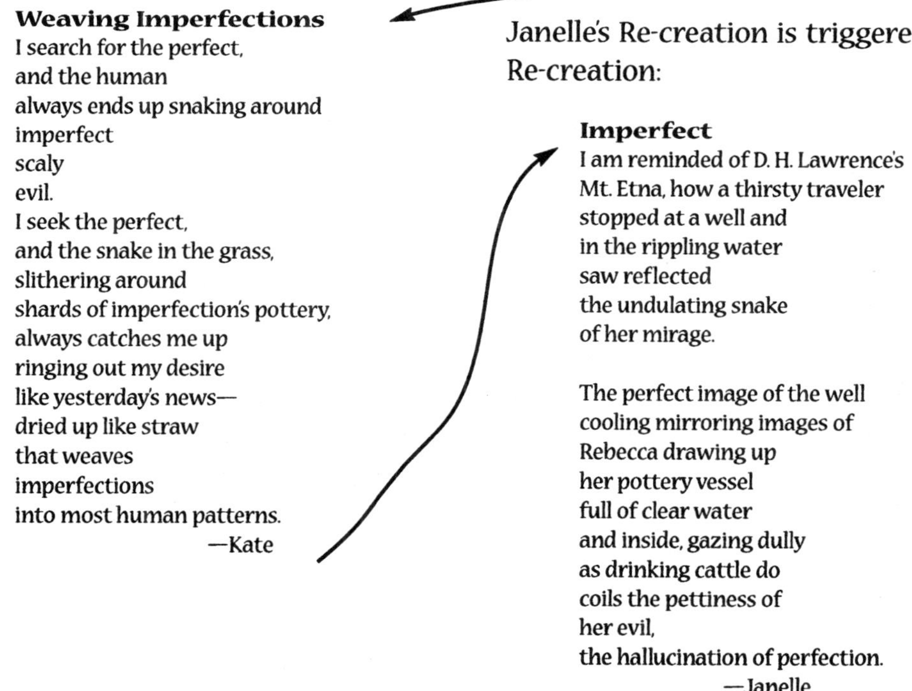

Weaving Imperfections
I search for the perfect,
and the human
always ends up snaking around
imperfect
scaly
evil.
I seek the perfect,
and the snake in the grass,
slithering around
shards of imperfection's pottery,
always catches me up
ringing out my desire
like yesterday's news—
dried up like straw
that weaves
imperfections
into most human patterns.
—Kate

Janelle's Re-creation is triggered by Kate's Re-creation:

Imperfect
I am reminded of D. H. Lawrence's
Mt. Etna, how a thirsty traveler
stopped at a well and
in the rippling water
saw reflected
the undulating snake
of her mirage.

The perfect image of the well
cooling mirroring images of
Rebecca drawing up
her pottery vessel
full of clear water
and inside, gazing dully
as drinking cattle do
coils the pettiness of
her evil,
the hallucination of perfection.
—Janelle

And the final set of examples is based on a Re-creation of Sharon Olds', *The Possessive* (p. 73):

Mine
Mine, mine, many most times many,
as if by mouthing the word 'mine,'
she could become forever mine
with her wispy hair and her
flattened falling breast
as if by saying mine, she could be mine.

Janelle's Re-creation follows:

Mine
Her voice is wispy
after radiation.
Could that really be
my mother's rise
and fall
of intonation
on the end
of the line
wisps rising
from open cankers
from the womb of her mouth
cut and sore
breaths
rising and falling
and she won't stop calling
to tell me
through the pain
rising and falling
that her thoughts
are always on mine.
—Janelle

What Happens in Iterative Creative Acts?

Consider what happens when we re-create a Re-creation. Anything we write moves us farther and farther into new territory and farther and farther away from the original. We open ourselves to creative leaps that need never stop. A progressive series of Re-creations transforms the original into a totally new creation. Has accomplished its purpose of striking the match of inspiration. Activates improvisation. Allows us to see that the mind is much more powerful than we assume it to be.

> Nature is not mechanical, its prodigy is not identity but resemblance, and its universe is not an assembly line but an incessant creation.
> —Wallace Stevens

Multilogue opens us to the mysteries of mind, makes us accept the uncertain nature of improvisation, enhances tolerance to other views, other ways of expression. Awareness of multilogue is often tacit rather than explicit. The Re-creations follow gradations from similarities to the original to totally different. In the middle lies an admixture, a mingling and a fusion, creating a new texture, a new context, an interbreeding of two—or more—minds, not to mention the context of the culture. The writer's mind, flavored by the original, takes off in its own direction. The joining of the thing and the thing heard creates a third thing, the Re-creation, and then another, and then another. The result is a symbiosis, an interlinking, a coalescence of minds, an alliance between poet and hearer, between student and student, between writer and writer— a new expressive articulation.

Our relationship to something to be learned changes from being only a *spectator* to being a *participant* in the creation of meaning, and, at its highest level, to being a creator. We are moved to action, involving us at a creative level so that we can produce our own configurations in the real world on a real page.

Going from Here: From Play to Dance to Collaborative Re-creations:

The means of getting to the core, essence, germ, the heart of something to be learned is rarely available—unless we are exposed to much coaching and testing—to those of us considered *ordinary.*

When I was teaching the play, *Oedipus Rex*, to a group of general education students who had no interest in taking this course except to get their requirement over , I showed a film of a dance interpretation by modern dancer, Martha Graham, of the play. Entitled *Night Journey* (1958), the performance focused on the moment of Jocasta's suicide with flashbacks to key events of the play unraveling the mystery. The only other dancers were Oedipus, the blind seer, Tiresias, and the Greek Chorus. Students were fascinated by the compression of images, by the translation of the story into movement, by the wordlessness of the Re-creation of the Sophocles play. Immediately after the viewing, I asked them to re-create Martha Graham' interpretation in groups of four. The only criterion was that they accomplish their interpretation in the three-line syllabics of Haiku: five syllables, seven syllables, five syllables. They had 10 minutes to work collaboratively. This is what emerged:

Angles and elbows,
quick movements linger in time.
Jocasta dances.

The king lost his sight
Jocasta swings from the cord.
Mother and son — NO!

Destiny and Fate.
Always two ends of a rope
will remain, though cut.

Jocasta attempts
to escape that which fooled none:
Wife/mother of Fate.

The blind seer tapped truth.
The proud king sought culprits.
Jocasta's light dawned.

One rebellious group ignored the haiku format, coming up with a *suicide note* instead:

Dear Oedipus:
Well, it was good while it lasted—at least the kids are healthy, no genetic defects or anything. Listen, you keep the castle, the Chorus, the kids. I'm outta here. Just want you to know, it was good while it lasted. Love, Jo

What We Can Learn from the Interlinking Process of Re-creations

To make the insights of this book useable, let's recap. We can learn as spectators, the most heavily passive way of learning, though it is often practical and convenient and testable. We can learn as participants; it is much more animating, less tidy, less controllable. Then we can learn as creators, each charting our own learning curve, but building, always on the guidance of the past, the doing of the present, the projecting into an unknown future, an unknown moment that may or may not be eloquent or useful. At other times in human history, the move into the unknown was not safe, so it was better to transmit past knowledge as a way to control the eternal unknown. In the now and the future twenty-first century, given technological advances and accessibility of knowledge bases, pure transmission as a primary vehicle of learning has become obsolete. Participation as a secondary mode is insufficient. The emphasis of learner as creator, risker, knower that life is always uncertain, that knowledge is unstable, that life has to be improvised, especially in turbulent times, is key to human growth and development.

What we need to build into our learning curve in formal educational settings: Ways to contract/expand. We already know how to contract; it is a built-in safety mechanism. It is more difficult to expand. Expanding demands flexibility and risk-taking. Contracting into the known is retreating to previous learned behaviors, many of which do not work in the new millennium.

The more there is to know, the more we need to know, and the more we, as individuals, have to go through cultural evolution before pushing the envelope further. Knowledge is not as fixed as we would like it to be. In fact, the world is not stable and fixed as we would like it to be. We need skills to choose and choose rapidly. Re-creations give concrete feedback to help use our brains in improvisational ways and therefore to hone our underused intuitive edge of knowing.

The key value of Re-creations is its making visible and concrete the reach for the creative in order to transcend how we are, where we are, what we are. It is a way to become aware of—and to embrace— the multi-perspectives within ourselves as well as in the world external to us, to be able to put ourselves in the place of the other and to empathize, as well as to realize, that our experiences are universal.

A Re-creation becomes a reciprocal give and take between: the shock of the new, unpredictable data, sudden emotions, divergence— we change as we participate. The energy generated nudges us to a higher level of understanding. Self transcendence leads to greater connection with ourselves, with others, and ultimately with what it means to be human.

Reflective Awareness of Process:

The sense of evolving pattern as we progress through self-similar series of levels becomes a self-reflexive, self-conscious act of learning, helping us to recognize our natural adaptive skills. Creative bricolage, the selection and recombination of sounds, images, ideas, letting them overlap, be juxtaposed, allows us to become participants in an ever-evolving unfolding of creative expressions in favor of mere *appreciation* or rote learning. Ideas, images, stories, sounds—indeed, all patterns—migrate. Humans desire above all, a predictable and ordered world, a world to which they are securely oriented. But because humans desire such a world so passionately, they are inclined to ignore anything that intimates that they do not know it, understand it. We tend to ascribe negative value to anything disorienting, anything that requires us to experience cognitive tension. Art—the poem, the painting, the dance—reinforces the capacity to endure disorientation.

Art keeps us aware that our brains are grounded in uncertainty (Prigogine)and that for that very reason our minds are capable of surprise, of improvisation, of innovation. "Art," writes biologist Morse Peckham, " is rehearsal for the orientation which makes innovation possible." And, in formal schooling, we are rarely given the opportunity to rehearse in order to remember and be more aware of, this mental gift.

> Art is a necessity, the astounding human evolutionary and cultural development would not have been possible without it.
>
> —Morse Peckham

Cognitive tension must be experienced as a dominant feeling before a problem can be defined, before a Re-creation can occur, before something new can be entertained. Because our right brain thinks, not logically but analogically, not by deductive steps but by observing similarities and dissimilarities between remembered patterns and new ones, we are capable of improvisation. We are capable of re-creating the art of others to create new coherences in our own minds.

> Without invention nothing is well spaced,
> unless the mind change, unless
> the stars are new measured, according
> to their relative positions, the
> line will not change, the necessity
> will not matriculate: unless there is
> a new mind there cannot be a new
> line, the old will go on
> repeating itself with recurring
> deadliness… .
>
> —William Carlos Williams
> from Paterson

Re-creations not only modulate, they alter, permutate,variegate, depart from, diverge from, diversify. These permutations serve as the springboard to engage us in creative acts of our own.

The Affect-Link: What Happens When we Aren't Permitted to Create

The key to creative acts is the affect-link. Expression. A sense of satisfaction and pleasure in the doing. That is what its negative pole is all about when human beings don't know they have a creative voice, thus acting out destructively to make a statement. As human beings, our primary strength is the flexibility of our brain, and our brains must be flexible enough to incorporate our prior experience without getting stuck in patterns of habitual, programmed behavior. Our brains must be flexible enough to transcend our prior experiences in order not to die or to kill or be stuck or to be relegated to extinction.

Amazingly, the human brain has evolved, for whatever reason, to be flexible enough not only to transcend genetic programming but to incorporate, in constructive ways, the lessons of the past. The human brain has survived by learning to become creative in the face of insurmountable obstacles, in discovering ways to move beyond the given, the set, the programmed, the fixed, the rule-bound, the finite, the material to discover, via combinatory play, the virtual, the bricolage, the generated ensemble, the re-programmed, the crazy connection, the unlikely match, the surprise—always the surprise.

Flexibility has moved the human mind into the macrocosm of possibility, that is, into the realm of the creative, the new combination, the odd connection, the synthesis of what has gone before. In microcosm, such leaps, synthesizing moves, connections, associations, mergers, are made manifest in the phenomenon of Re-creations. In microcosm, Re-creations show us what human beings are capable of when they dare to—are allowed to, are encouraged to go beyond the rule-governed, the limits, (verbal or otherwise), the expected. Re-creations remind us that the human is first and foremost a creative, communicating, expressive, vortex of possibility, and that this is the human's forte, not hide nor hair nor teeth nor eyes nor nose nor speed—but a brain that can learn and learn and learn, thereby transcending all that has gone before without rejecting it but by incorporating that which will lead to a new synthesis.

Re-creations are a way of helping ordinary human beings experience that human impulse. They are a way of helping us to know the moment of going beyond the known, the moment of risking, going beyond the critical censor which says, "I can't/don't know how/haven't got the skill." At the same time it shows us, reminds us, lets us build upon, whatever human knowing, we can cling to in our little life. It strengthens the human ability to move between two poles: The mental interplay between the big picture—the vision, the sense of the whole, the intuitive— and the particular, the detail, the steps, the how to, the use of tools such as language or hammers and chisels or math or literature—even the poem created by another creator who has gone before us and who has dared to express the inexpressible.

Each time we express, we transcend ourselves. At the same time, each time we incorporate the images, ideas, sounds, movements, inventions, of those who have gone before us, we make that transcendence more palpable, more communicable, more real, more buildable, more functional, more expressive. Each time we are given an opportunity to express ourselves as creative human beings, we experience the heart of our humanness.

Epilogue

Human beings have created and re-created from their first stirrings as verbal creatures, where they could externalize by expressing and passing on and utilizing the known, yet moving beyond the known to risk the new, the unexpected. That is the meaning of the word CREATIVE, it is to make or do beyond that has gone before. That cumulative creative effort depends on moving beyond the shared knowledge, of proving that shared knowledge can be reorganized, synthesized into ever self-similar—though not identical—patterns of meaning.

Each individual, each generation, each culture, simultaneously transcends and incorporates what has gone before. And must do so. The greater our communication skills and vehicles, the greater our multilogue, our chorus of voices that continues to sound the different drummer, the unique voices.

Human knowing, human knowledge, human skill, have expanded so dramatically because the incorporating has been speeded up by the new technology that humans have devised, always standing on the shoulders of giants—and, certainly, and less conspicuously, standing on each others' shoulders.

Re-creation is nothing more than an immediate process which allows us to become conscious of our improvisational gifts—of adapting, joining, improving, inspiring, re-creating what has gone before into the new. This flexible gift of the human must be nurtured, experienced, exploited, exhibited, sampled, exampled—always—to the learners among us. In a flexible world, this potential is open to us all, to each human being, to each mind, to each culture, to each generation, each time in more expansive, more vital ways.

All invention is Re-creation of what has gone before. All verbal or visual Re-creations build on the slender thread of human thought, imagination, vision, playfulness, even bodily stamina, thus transcending previous limits. (Every famous athlete—Jordan, Sosa, McGwire— has done nothing more than transcend the limits set before without rejecting the power and strength and skill of those who have gone before; those gifts have not only been transcended, they have been incorporated.)

> Finished persons are very common—people often are closed up, quite satisfied that there is little or nothing more to learn.
> —Robert Henri

> There is no limit to the new kinds of things that can come into being, to the number of transformations, both qualitative and quantitative, that can occur. The ideas come first. The mythos leads the logos.
>
> —Alfred North Whitehead

Conclusion to the Whole Book:

Re-creations result in a profusion of variation, not imitation, not copy, not facsimile, transcript, not parody, not paraphrase, not translation, not even similitude, but transformation of an original,

Many of us still assume that meaning is knowable because it is stable. The truth is that meaning is dynamic, in ongoing revision, transformation, transmutation, mutation each time a conversation takes place. The metaphor of the mirror image does not hold. The metaphor of on-going iteration of meaning, comes much closer to how human beings formulate images, thoughts, ideas, words, language to MEAN something, even if it is tentative, improvisational, surprising. Ever since human beings started to story, sing, and draw, they have re-designed, re-created, re-invented, have made new the old, have personalized the *other* in order to assimilate it and make it.

> Re-creations give you a voice so you're not separate from the poet's voice; you feel as though you were the poet speaking, yet it is your own voice.
>
> —Student

> Art is a mystery. A mystery is something immeasurable. Insofar as every child and woman and man may be immeasurable, art is the mystery of every man and woman and child. Insofar as a human being is an artist, skies and mountains and oceans and thunderbolts and butterflies are immeasurable; and art is every mystery of nature. Nothing measurable can be alive; nothing which is not alive can be art.
>
> —e. e. cummings

B•I•B•L•I•O•G•R•A•P•H•Y

Arendt, Hannah. *Amazon*..

Ashton, Dore, *Picasso on Art: A Selection of Views*, NY: Viking, 1972

Ayrton, Michael, *The Rudiments of Paradise*. New York: Weybright and Talley. 1971.

Barron, Frank, *No Rootless Flower: The Ecology of Creativity*. 1995

Berry, Wendell. *Openings*. NY: Harcourt Brace Jovanovich, Inc. 19__

Bly, Robert, ed. *Neruda and Vallejo: Selected Poems*.

Bogen, Joseph E. "one Brain, or Two, or Both?" *In Two Hemispheres, One Brain?* ed. F. Lepore, et. al. NY: Allan Liss, 1990

Bogen, Joseph E., "Split Brains: Interhemispheric Exchange as a Source of Creativity." In M. A. Runco and S. Pritzker (eds). *Encyclopedia of Creativity*. 1998

Bowen, Elizabeth. *The Collected Stories of Elizabeth Bowen*. Ecco Press. 1996.

Bradbury, Ray, *Zen in the Art of Writing*. NY: Bantam Books. 1990

Brand, Alice, and Richard Graves, eds ." *Presence of Mind: Writing and the Domain Beyond the Cognitive*. Brand, Alice and Dick Graves. Portsmouth, NH: Heinemann/Boynton-Cook. 1992.

Britton, James. "Talking and Writing." In Eldonna Evertts, ed. *Explorations in Children's Writing*. Illinois: NCTE. 1970

Brooks, Gwendolyn, *Blacks*. Harper Collins 1987

Carter, Jared. "Improvisation." from *Les Barricades Mysterieuses*: OH: Cleveland State U. 1999

Catacalos, Rosemary, in *Discoverin. Literature*. Second ed.

Chasin, Helen, *Casting Stones*. NY: Little, Brown 1975 OR *Coming Close*. CT: Yale University Press. 1968

Ciardi, John. *Live Another Day*. NY: Twayne, 1949

Csikszentmihalyi, Mihaly, Creativity: *Flow and the Psychology of Discovery and Invention*. 1996.

Damasio, Antonio, *The Feeling of What Happens*. NY: Putnam. 1999

Eliot, T. S., "Tradition and Individual Talent." *Selected Essays 1917-1932* NY: Harcourt, Brace, 1932

Eliot, T. S. , *Collected Poems 1909-1962*. London: Faber and Faber.

Einstein, Albert. in Brewster Ghiselin, ed. *The Creative Process*. NY: New American Library, 1955

Ferlinghetti, Lawrence. *When I Look at Pictures*. Salt Lake City: Peregrine Smith Books. 1990.

Field, Joanna, *An Experiment in Leisure*. NY: Putnam.1937

Field, Joanna, *On Not Being Able to Paint*. NY: Putnam.

Fuller, Renee. *In Search of the IQ Correlation*. NY: Ball-Stick-Bird Publications. 1977

Frost, Robert. *The Poetry of Robert Frost*. NY: Holt, Rinehart and Winston 1952

Frye, Northrop. (see Amazon.com

Fuller, Renee, *In Search of the IQ Correlation*. Ball-Stick-Bird Publications. 1974

Gardner, Howard, *Creating Minds*. NY: Basic Books. 1993.

Geertz, Clifford. *The Interpretation of Cultures*. New York: Basic Books. 1973

Gelernter, David. *The Muse in the Machine*: *Computerizing the Poetry of Human Thought*. NY: The Free Press. 1994.

Gerard, R. W. "The Biological Basis of Imagination." in Brewster Ghiselin, ed. *The Creative Process*. New York: The New American Library. 1952

Gilbert, Judy, *Clear Speech*. Boston: Cambridge University Press, 1993

Goethe, Johann Wolfgang von. Amazon.com

Goldberg, Philip, Tarcher Public on *Peak Performance*
Goleman, Daniel, Paul Kaufman, Michael Ray, *The Creative Spirit*. NY:Plume. 1993.
Hass, Robert. *Field Guide*. Yale University Press 1973
Hayden, Robert. *Angle of Ascent, New and Selected Poems*. Liveright Publishing Corp. 1975
Henri, Robert .
Hopkins, Gerard Manley.
Houston, Jean. *The Possible Human*. Los Angeles: Jeremy Tarcher, 1982
Huidobro, Vincente. *The Selected Poetry of Vincente Huidobro*. New Directions 1981
Kunitz, Stanley. *Next-to-Last Things*. NY: Atlantic Monthly, 1985
Lorde, Audre, "Poems Are Not Luxuries." In Donald Hall, ed. *Claims for Poetry*. 1982
Kincaid, James R. "Purloined Letters." *The New Yorker*. 93-97. January 20, 1997.
James, William. *Varieties of Religious Experience*. Cambridge, MA: Harvard University Press, 1985
Johnston, Charles M., *The Creative Imperative*. Berkeley: Celestial Arts. 1986.
Joyce, James, *The Dubliners*.
Justice, Donald. *New and Selected Poems*. New York: Alfred A. Knopf. 1995.
Langer, Susanne, *Problems of Art*. New York: Charles Scribner's Sons. 1957
Lorde, Audre, "Poems Are Not Luxuries."
Lorenz, Konrad, *Analogy as a Source of Knowledge*. Science, 1974, 185. 229-234.
Mailer, Norman. *Portrait of Picasso as a Young Man*. NY: The Atlantic Monthly Press. 1995.
Millay, Edna St. Vincent. *Collected Poems*. NY: Harper & Row 1923
Mueller, Lisel, *The Need to Hold Still*. Baton Rouge: Louisiana State University Press. 1981
__________ *Alive Together*. Baton Rouge: Louisiana State University Press. 1996.
Nachmanovitch, Stephen, *Free Play*. Los Angeles: Jeremy P. Tarcher. 1990
Neruda, Pablo. "Childhood and Poetry" from Robert Bly, *Neruda and Vallejo*. Boston: Beacon Press. 1971
Olds, Sharon, "The Possessive" from *Satan Says*. PA: University of Pittsburgh Press 1980
Oliver, Mary, *New and Selected Poems*. Beacon Press 1992.
Ostriker, Alicia, *The Crack in Everything*. Pennsylvania: University of Pittsburgh Press 1996
__________, *Nakedness of the Fathers*. Rutgers University Press, 1994
__________, *The Imaginary Lover*.
Owen, Wilfred. *The Collected Poems of Wilfred Owen*. London: Chatto and Windus, Ltd. 1963
Pastan, Linda. *Heroes in Disguise*. NY: W. W. Norton & Company, Inc. 1991
Paz, Octavio. *A Draft of Shadows*. The New Yorker Magazine. 1975
Peckham, Morse.
Peirce, C. S. *Collected Papers* (Vols. I-VI) Cambridge: Harvard University Press. 1934
Piercy, Marge. *Circles on the Water*. NY: Alfred A. Knopf, Inc. 1982
Pinker, Stephen, *How the Mind Works*. NY: Norton. 1997
Poincare, Henri. "Mathematical Creation." in Brewster Ghiselin, ed. *The Creative Process*. New York: The New American Library. 1952
Polanyi, Michael. *The Tacit Dimension*. Magnolia, MA: Peter Smith, 1983.
Prigogine, Ilya, *From Being to Becoming*. NY: W. H. Freeman, 1980
Richards, M. C. , *Centering: Poetry, Pottery, and the Person*. CT: Wesleyan University Press, 1964
Rico, Gabriele, *Writing the Natural Way*, second edition, NY: Penguin/Putnam. 2000
__________, "The Heart of the Matter: Language, Feeling, Stories, Healing." *Presence of Mind: Writing and the Domain Beyond the Cognitive*. Brand, Alice and Dick Graves, eds. Portsmouth, NH: Heinemann/Boynton-Cook. 1992.
__________, *Pain and Possibility: Writing Your Way through Personal Crisis*. Penguin/Putnam 1991.
__________, "Reading for Non-Literal Meaning." In *Reading, the Arts, and the Creation of Meaning*. Elliot Eisner, ed. Reston, VA: The National Art Education Association. 1978
Robison, Mary. "Yours." From *An Amateur's Guide to the Night*. NY: Alfred A. Knopf, Inc. 1981
Sexton, Anne. *All My Pretty Ones*. Boston: Houghton Mifflin Co. 1962

Shank, Roger, *Tell Me a Story: A New Look at Real and Artificial Memory*, NY: Scribner's. 1990.
Shank, Roger, *The Creative Attitude: Learning to Ask and Answer the Right Questions.* NY: Macmillan.1988
Shlain. Leonard, *The Alphabet and the Goddess: The Conflict between Word and Image.* NY:Viking 1998
Simon, Maurya. *The Enchanted Room.* Copper Canyon Press. 1989
Stafford, William, *Passwords.* NY: Harper 1991.
Siler, Todd. *Think Like a Genius.* NY: Bantam. 1996
Sternberg, R. *Defying the Crowd: Cultivating Creativity in a Culture of Conformity.* NY: The Free Press, 1995
Stevens, Wallace, *The Necessary Angel.* NY: my shelves
Wagoner, David. *Collected Poems 1956-1976.* IN: Indiana University Press 1976
Wagoner, David. *First Light.* NY: Little, Brown and Co.
Wheateley, Margaret. *A Simpler Way.*
Williams, C. K. *Poems 1983-1983.* NY: Farrar, Strauss, and Giroux 1969
Wolff, Tobias. *This Boy's Life.* NY: Atlantic Monthly Press, 1989.
Young, Al. *The Blues Don't Change.* Louisiana State University Press 1965

I • N • D • E • X

T

W

Y

PERMISSIONS

Wendell Berry. "The Peace of Wild Things" from *Openings*. Copyright 1968 by Wendell Berry. Reprinted by permission of Harcourt Brace Jovanovich, Inc.
Gwendolyn Brooks. "Hunchback Girl" and "The Chicago Picasso." From *Blacks* by Gwendolyn Brooks. Reprinted by permission of HarperCollins.
Jared Carter. "Improvisation." Reprinted by permission of Cleveland State University, Ohio.
Rosemary Catacalos. "La Casa" from *Again for the First Time*,. Copyright 1984. Reprinted by permission of the author.
Helen Chasin. "The Word Plum." Copyright 1968 by Helen Chasin. Reprinted by permission of AMS Press.
John Ciardi. "Sometimes Running." From *The Collected Poems of John Ciardi*. Copyright 1997. Reprinted by permission of The University of Arkansas Press.
Billy Collins. "Introduction to Poetry." Reprinted by permission of The University of Arkanasas Press. Copyright 1988 by Billy Collins.
Louis Corinth. "Carmencita." Reproduced by permission of Staedesches Kunst Intitut Frankfurt am Main.
Philip Dacey. "Proofreading" from *The Deathbed Playboy* by Philip Dacey. Copyright 1999 by Philip Dacey. Reprinted by permission of Eastern Washington University Press..
T.S. Eliot. "Preludes" from *Collected Poems 1909-1962* by T.S. Eliot. Reprinted by permission of the p ublishers, Faber & Faber, Ltd.,
Lawrence Ferlinghetti. "Short Story on a Painting of Gustav Klimt" from *A Coney Island of the Mind*. Copyright 1958 by Lawrence Ferlinghetti. Reprinted by permission of New Directions Publishing Corporation.
Robert Frost. "Nothing Gold Can Stay" from *Poetry of Robert Frost: The Collected Poems*. Copyright 1979. Reprinted by permission of Henry Holt & Co.
Nan Fry. "The Plum" from *Relearning the Dark*. Copyright 1991 by Nan Fry. Reprinted by permission of the Washington Writers' Publishing House.
Robert Haas. "Song" from *Field Guide* by Robert Haas. Reprinted by permission of Yale University Press.
Robert Hayden. "Those Winter Sundays." Reprinted from *Angle of Ascent, New & Selected Poems* by Robert Hayden. By permission of Liveright Publishing Corporation. Copyright 1975 by Robert Hayden.
Hokusai. "The Great Wave." Work is in the public domain.
Vicente Huidobro. "Ars Poetica" from *The Selected Poetry of Vicente Huidobro*, W..S. Marwin, trans. Reprinted by permission of New Directions Publishing Corporation.
Donald Justice. "Men at Forty" from Night Light . Copyright 1981 by Donald Justice. University Press of New England. Reprinted by permission of the University Press of New England.
Lincoln Kirstein. "Tchelitchev." 1994. Reproduced by permission of Twelvetress Press, Santa Fe, New Mexico.
Gustav Klimt. "The Kiss." Reproduced by permission of the Osteroreichische Galerie Belvedere, Vienna, Austria.
Stanley Kunitz. "The Scene" from *The Wild Card: Selected Poems, 1998*. Reprinted by permission of University of Illinois Press.
Teo Lei. "Respect." The poem is in the public domain.
Denise Levertov "Writing in the Dark" from *Breaking the Water*. Copyright 1987 by Denise Levertov. Reprinted by permission of New Directions Publishing Corporation.
Audre Lorde. "Poems Are Not Luxuries" Copyright 1982 by Audre Lorde. Reprinted by permission of the author.
Marjorie Maddox. "Elocution Lessons" from *College English*, 1994. Copyright 1994 by Marjorie Maddox. Reprinted by permission of The National Council of Teachers of English.
Edna St. Vincent Millay. "An Ancient Gesture" from *Collected Poems*. HarperCollins. Copyright 1954, 1982 by Norma Millay Ellis. All rights reserved. Reprinted by permission of Elizabeth Barnett, literary executor.
Piet Mondrian. "The Painting." Reprinted by permission of the Museum of Modern Art, New York.
Lisel Mueller. "The Story How Fire Took Water to Wife" from *Alive Together* by :Lisel Mueller. Reprinted by permission of Louisiana State University Press.
Edvard Munch. "The Scream." Reproduced by permission of the Museum of Fine Arts, Boston, Massachusetts.
Pablo Neruda. *Neruda & Vallejo - Selected Poems 1962*. John Knoepfle, trans., copyright 1972. Reprinted by permission of Beacon Press.
Sharon Olds. "For My Daughter" from *The Dead and the Living*. Copyright 1973 by Sharon Olds. Alfred A. Knopf. Reprinted by permission of the author.
Sharon Olds. "The Possessive" from *Satan Says*. Copyright 1980 by Sharon Olds. University of Pittsburgh Press. Reprinted by permission of the author.
Mary Oliver. "When Death Comes" from *New and Selected Poems by Mary Oliver*. Copyright 1992 by Mary Oliver. Reprinted by permission of Beacon Press, Boston Massachusetts.
Mary Oliver. "The Black Snake" from *Twelve Moons* by Mary Oliver. Copyright 1978 by Mary Oliver. Reprinted by permission of Little Brown and Co.
Alicia Suskin Ostriker. "Dissolve in Slow Motion" from *The Crack in Everything*. Copyright 1996. Reprinted by permission of the University of Pittsburgh Press. (Thisted in many sources to Adrienne Rich).
Wilfred Owen. "Dulce at Decorum Est" from *The Collected Poems of Wildred Owen*. Copyright 1963 by Chatto and Windus, Ltd. Reprinted by permission of New Directions Publishing.
Linda Pastan. "1932" from *Heroes in Disguise* by Linda Pastan. Copyright 1991 by Linda Pastan. Reprinted by permission of W.W. Norton & Co.
Linda Pastan. "To a Daughter Leaving Home" from *Carnival Evening: New and Selected Poems 1968-1998* by Linda Pastan. Copyright 1998 by Linda Pastan. Reprinted by permission of W.W. Norton & Co.
Linda Pastan. "Posterity" from *Heroes in Disguise*. Copyright 1991 by Linda Pastan. Reprinted by permission of W.W. Norton & Co..
Octavio Paz. "Wind, Water and Stone" by Octavio Paz, translation by Mark Strand, from *Collected Poems 1957-1987*. Copyright 1979 by *The New Yorker Magazine*. Reprinted by permission of New Directions Publising Corporation.
Pablo Picasso. "Portrait of a Painter After El Greco." Reprinted by permission of the Museo De Bellas Artes, Sevilla.
Marge Piercy. "Simple Song" from *Circles on the Water*. Copyright 1982 by Marge Piercy. Alfred A. Knopf. Reprinted by permission of the author.
Mary Robison. "Yours" from *An Amateur's Guide to the Night: Stories*. Copyright 1989 by Mary Robison. Reprinted by permission of publisher David R. Godine.
Roelant Savery. "Orpheus unter den Tieren." Reproduced by permission of Staedesches Kunst Institut Frankfurt am Main.
Otto Franz Schloderer. "Der Geiger am Fenster." Reproduced by permission of Staedesches Kunst Institut Frankfurt am Main.
Anne Sexton. "To a Friend Whose Work Has Come to Triumph" from *All My Pretty Ones*. Copyright 1962 by Anne Sexton. Renewed 1990 by Linda G. Sexton. Reprinted by permission of Houghton Mifflin Co. All rights reserved.
Maurya Simon. "Women at Thirty" Copyright 1989 by Maurya Simon. Reprinted by permssion of Copper Canyon Press.
David Wagoner. "The Other House" from *First Light*. Copyright 1983 by David Wagoner. Little Brown and Co. Reprinted by permission of the author.
David Wagoner. "The Old Words" from *Collected Poems 1956-1976*. Copyright 1976 by David Wagoner. Indiana University Press. Reprinted by permission of the author.
C.K. Williams. "Hood" from *Poems 1963-1983*. Copyright 1988 by C.K. Williams. Reprinted by permission of Farrar, Straus & Giroux, LLC.
Al Young. "Chemistry" from *The Blues Don't Change*. Copyright 1981 by Lousiana State University Press. Reprinted by permission of the author.

Also by
Gabriele Rico

Writing the Natural Way, 2nd ed.

Pain and Possibility: Writing Your Way through Personal Crisis

Designing Essays (with Kate Evans and Janelle Melvin)

Western Literature: Themes and Writers (with G. Robert Carlson)

Living Literature: Beginnings (with Hans Guth)

Discovering Literature: Stories, Poems, Plays (with Hans Guth)

Discovering Fiction (with Hans Guth)

Discovering Poetry (with Hans Guth)

Balancing the Hemispheres: Brain Research and the Teaching of Writing (with M. Claggett)

Garantiert Schreiben Lernen

Von der Seele Schreiben

To Write is to Know (audiotape)

Writing the Natural Way CD-Rom

For information and/or ordering, please contact

Gabriele Rico's website: gabrielerico.com or
writingthenaturalway.com

Creative Explorer, a software program - FAX 312 222-9024

CD Rom to accompany Writing the Natural Way - FAX 312 222-9024